The Power of One

Men and Women of Faith Who Make a Difference

THE POWER OF ONE

Men and Women of Faith Who Make a Difference

Edited by James L. Merrell

The Bethany Press
SAINT LOUIS   MISSOURI

© 1976 by The Bethany Press
All rights reserved. No part of this book may be reproduced by any method without the publisher's written permission. Address The Bethany Press, Box 179, St. Louis, Mo. 63166.

Scripture quotations, unless otherwise noted, are from the Revised Standard Version of the Bible, copyrighted 1946 and 1952 by the Division of Christian Education, National Council of Churches of Christ in the United States of America, and used by permission.

Library of Congress Cataloging in Publication Data

Merrell, James L.   1930-
   The Power of One

   Includes bibliographical references.
   1. Christian biography. I. Title.
BR1700.2.P68   248'.6   76-16064
ISBN 0-8272-2925-9

Cover art by Terri Kurtz

MANUFACTURED IN THE UNITED STATES OF AMERICA

Contents

	page
Jean Christenson: Easing Aches in Appalachia	11
Sherrill Milnes: Amazing Grace at the Met	17
Raymon B. Fogg: Hope After the Hurricane	23
"The Lady": She Reached Out with Love	27
Testimony of Hope: He Makes Today Count	30
Mr. Smith of Brown Creek: Teaching Lessons to the Preacher	34
Uncle Gus: Legacy of a Last Reunion	40
Feeding the Hungry: She Heard God Say "Go!"	43
Alex Gilmore: Making Friends for the Church	47
Rhea Zakich: A Riot Set Her Faith on Fire	50
Ron Schipper: More Than a Football Coach	54
A Monday Morning Writer of Letters: Words Can Make a Difference	57
Jan Gallagher: Mission on a Motorcycle	60
Edward L. Rada: Building a Bridge Across the Pacific	65
Single Parent: Finding a Place in the Big City	70
Lillian Willoughby: Turning the Other Cheek Means Caring	76
Christopher Ballard: A Child's Gift of Joy	80
Eddie Aguilar: Another Kind of Revolution	84
Lydia Dowler: God Makes a Task Possible	88
A Congregation: No Excuses—Just Action	92
One Family: Finding Joy in the Midst of Loss	96
Judith Cox: God Shapes Her Destiny	106
Dorothy Russell: A Mighty Mite Who Mends Men	108
At Work in a Nursing Home	113
Easter People	118
Thank You, God, for . . .	121

I am only one,
But still I am one.
I cannot do everything,
But still I can do something;
And because I cannot do everything
I will not refuse to do the
  something that I can do.

—EDWARD EVERETT HALE

PREFACE

A verse by Edward Everett Hale (1822-1909) may still be quoted occasionally today, but it has lost much of its impact.

> I am only one,
> But still I am one.
> I cannot do everything,
> But still I can do something. . . .

The clergyman-editor, author of *The Man Without a Country*, believed that a solitary individual could "do something" to change the world for the better.

How many would agree with Hale today?

This is an era of massive and bewildering human problems. What can "only one" do about global starvation, ecological deterioration or international political tension? How can a lone individual add constructively to the search for freedom and justice, or help turn the tide of enlarging selfishness, cynicism and despair?

Hale's poetic optimism, many would feel, belongs to an earlier, more simple time—before we spoke routinely of transnational corporations, a Third (and even Fourth) World, racial, ethnic and sexual blocs, oil politics and space exploration.

Most persons would question whether any one man or woman could do what governments, armies, corporations or large-scale and costly programs have attempted and have often failed to accomplish.

Yet the poet may have the correct view of things.

The inability of the world to solve its agonizing problems at some high and overarching level—with a "bigness" to match the dimensions of the challenges—should cause us to look again at the way change really takes place.

The real center of transforming power remains the same in this century as in previous ones. It is in the mind, soul, and hands of each individual.

It is naïve to discount the realities in our contemporary world and to assert that legislation, diplomacy, structural reform, and tax demands somehow will fade into the background and no longer be priorities once individual morality and courage are sufficiently multiplied. Yet it is just as simplistic and wrong to believe that all problems can be solved if ample laws can be added to the books, technological advances made and grand programs instituted.

It is the *individual* who holds the key.

Dramatic changes can take place when men and women believe in the possibilities for human fulfillment, care about their world, and become involved where they are.

Likewise, humanity stumbles and suffers its way toward self-destruction when few persons are motivated enough to shout, "This will not happen!"

The tragedy of our time can be linked to our failure at this basic, personal level. It is not our science or our possessions that have failed us. Ours is a *human* problem. Too many persons are apathetic, discouraged, defeated, numbed. Too many have lost any awareness of right and wrong. Millions live only for themselves and have only a laissez-faire attitude toward those who brutalize and exploit.

Individual power determines the course of human affairs, and our plight today results from the misuse, neglect, and misdirection of that incredible force.

But there are other stories that should be told.

In every community there are men and women who, prompted by the assurances and demands of the Christian gospel, are making their lives count.

Most of these individuals are ordinary persons who do not hold prestigious positions of authority or responsibility. They do not often make headlines or give autographs. They are not credited with historic victories over the age-old enemies of humankind.

But as they go about the hard, frustrating daily job of living they touch others around them in a positive way—listening, healing, lifting, loving, reconciling, challenging, redeeming.

This book presents several stories of persons who are bringing Edward Everett Hale's words to life in our own time.

Here are men and women who, even though they "cannot do everything," are able to "do something." Like all of us, they have special gifts and unique opportunities which are being used to bring light into a darkened, pessimistic, insensitive world.

The church press traditionally has sought out human-interest stories, so it is from the pages of several major Catholic and Protestant journals that the chapters of this book are drawn.

All sorts of persons are represented here. We hope that the reader will find several sketches that will serve as mirrors for reflection, self-assessment, and commitment. If these persons can make an impact through their faith, should we not "go and do likewise"?

The religious journals represented in this book have enjoyed a long period of editorial fellowship and sharing through an informal association called Interchurch Features. Each of the stories published herein originated with one of the ICF publications, and many have appeared in other journals within the fellowship. Editors know that a good story has no denominational tag!

The chapters in this book have appeared in slightly different form in recent issues of *A.D., U.S. Catholic, The Disciple, The Episcopalian, The Lutheran, The Church Herald, The Observer, United Methodists Today,* and *Presbyterian Survey*. We are indebted to the editors and publishers of these major periodicals for their cooperation in this venture.

The anticipation is that these stories of faith will be a reminder of the awesome power that each of us possesses and will give readers a fresh determination to tackle those issues that many persons say are insoluble.

I am only one person.
I cannot do everything.
But I can do *something,* through the power of the living Christ at work in my life.

We will want to keep Edward Everett Hale's old favorite in our anthologies. Its words are appropriate even nearly a century later.

One person *has* power. And that power can be used to bring in a new order which Jesus described as the Kingdom.

James L. Merrell

Jean Christenson:

Easing Aches in Appalachia

by Floramae Geiser

The gray-haired woman seemed to be sleeping in her nursing-home bed. But the eyes popped open as we drew near.
"I'm not asleep," she said. "Hi, Chris. I'm glad you came."
With that Jean (Chris) Christenson introduced me to Mrs. Marie Heninger.

"This is my adopted daughter," Mrs. Heninger said with affection as she patted Chris's arm.

That was the kind of pride and love for Chris I witnessed often during the two days I traveled with this young woman who is ministering to the mountain folk of Appalachian Kentucky. They need her. And, she is quick to add, she needs them.

To visit Mary West, Chris and I turned off the country road and slid through red mud to park the car near a rustic woodframe house. We dashed through rain to the porch. As we scraped our shoes across the porch run, Mary came to the door to greet us with a wriggling year-old grandson in her arms.

"Don't worry none about mud," she said. "This is just a plain country home. We're used to mud."

Inside, the heat radiating from the black stove in the middle of the room felt good against the dampness.

We fussed over young Stevie. Then Mary talked to Chris about the sore throat that was troubling her.

"I can only take liquids now—can't stand to eat anything solid," said Mary. Chris asked a few questions, then recommended that Mary see the clinic doctor.

Reassured, Mary turned to me. "I don't know what I'd do without this girl. When I had my tonsils taken out last fall she took me to the hospital. And when I woke up, she was the first one there smiling at me.

"I tell you, I've lived 45 years and Chris is the best friend I've ever had.

"When Momma took so sick, Chris arranged to get her in the hospital. And after she died, Chris was around to help me out."

Mary talked about the high school equivalency test she had recently taken, hoping she'd passed. She had gone to school for months to prepare. She brought out her study books.

"You can tell which subject gives me the most trouble," she said, pointing to the well-thumbed English literature section.

"Now that the kids are old enough (four of her eight are still at home) I want to get a decent job. You know, $189 a month of public assistance just isn't enough. Don't get me wrong, I appreciate every penny I've gotten. But I want to earn my own way.

"I had my cousin plow my garden last week. But I was sure surprised when I went to buy seed potatoes and bean seeds. The price had gone up so I just couldn't afford to carry those seeds home."

As we drove away from Mary West's, Chris worried about Mary's sore throat. And she speculated as to how she could get some seed potatoes and bean seeds for Mary.

One-to-one ministry is Chris's specialty. She is sponsored by Redeemer Lutheran Church in Somerset, Kentucky. Some 6200 families are considered to be living at the poverty level in the three counties where she works. Illiteracy is high, reaching 30 percent in one of the counties.

Chris has been ministering for a year and a half. Before that she was a public health nurse for seven years.

"I started this work because I wanted to do something that would show why the church is relevant today," Chris explains.

"My ministry is a combination of social work, community development, and public health. I call myself an outreach worker. I make a lot of home visits which is what I dearly love doing. Most of the families I follow have health needs. Many need assistance in seeking avenues of help from community resources. Others just need someone to talk to.

"I have made emergency visits to homes. I go on trips to the doctor's office or health department with expectant mothers, new mothers and babies and young children. I go to hospitals to help admit a patient, to stay with someone having surgery, to linger in the lobby with a patient's family. I've visited people along the road, at the laundromat, and on downtown sidewalks. I've made visits to those who are chronically ill, bedridden, handicapped, aged, lonely, depressed."

When the Redeemer Lutheran Church council wrote the job description for their rural ministry they said they needed a "people advocate." Chris's work is funded by the Lutheran Church in America's lay associate program of the Division for Mission in North America. Those who give to that cause might well take pride in how Jean Christenson passes along their concerns. She's the next best thing to being there.

Chris is tall and winsome with a broad and frequent smile. She brushes back long, wavy hair and often pushes up wire-rim glasses that slide down on her nose—"I've got to get those fixed!"

It seems impossible than an easy-going young person from an Iowa farm, still so full of wonderment at the goodness of living, could have nearly nine years of professional experience. But her skillful way with people confirms her maturity.

She lives in the little community of Marshes Siding in a red brick building that was once a four-room school. Each of the rooms has been turned into a small five-room apartment. Chris's apartment is full of the things she likes—books, plants, and music.

Chris knows how to minister to all ages. Our visit to the Richard Early home proved that. Chris described Evelyn Early as "a truly wonderful friend who has given me so much.

"She's the kind of person who makes good use of community resources as she learns of them and, in turn, encourages her neighbors to take advantage of self-improvement opportunities, too.

"Evelyn is about my age," continued Chris. "She has had a lot of health problems with her family, but her ability to cope and her cheerfulness are absolutely remarkable. And she passes that resourcefulness along to her boys."

The Earlys have seven boys who are a part of their family; the eldest is in the service in Okinawa, the youngest, three years old. Two are Evelyn's brothers and three are Richard's children by a former marriage.

As we turned into the long lane that led to the Early's modest home and acreage, Chris explained that two of the boys were handicapped. Due to a birth defect, fourteen-year-old Sam's legs had been amputated. Lee, a thirteen-year-old Mongoloid child, suffered an accident a couple years ago which had paralyzed his legs.

Lee was lying in the sun in the grassy yard when we arrived, his braced legs stretched out behind him.

"Hi, Chris," he waved.

"How-dy," answered Chris in her adopted drawl.

David ran up to tell Chris how many push-ups he'd had to do at school that day. Lee demonstrated how many he could do. Talmadge quit chasing baby pigs and ran around through the gate to join us. Soon all the boys had gathered.

Each of the boys had something to tell Chris. Evelyn joined them on the grass and patiently awaited her turn to talk.

When the kids saw that one of my cameras produced instant pictures, they clamored for more and offered suggestions for subjects. At first I was uneasy about Sammy without legs. I didn't want to deliberately include or exclude him from the pictures. But he quickly put me at ease by walking over on his hands to pose with the group.

He asked Chris, "Do you think she'd like to take a picture of a half-boy, half-robot?"

The question was typical of Sam's acceptance of himself and pride in his accomplishments. The other boys were proud of him, too, as he came out on new, longer artificial legs and crutches to pose for pictures.

Evelyn talked to Chris about more surgery for Lee scheduled for the following Monday.

"The doctor thinks maybe he can get some movement back in those legs," she said with hope.

"Can you get to the hospital?" asked Chris.

"Well, I don't know," replied Evelyn. "The old station wagon still isn't fixed."

"I'll drive you to Lexington," volunteered Chris.

"That's just like her," Evelyn said to me. "Always there when you need her. I don't know what we'd do without Chris."

Later I asked Chris if sharing so many of the problems of her mountain friends was depressing.

"No," said Chris. "Life in the hills of Kentucky isn't all problems or altogether negative. In getting to know the people I've found so many positive, happy, really good things about their lives. And in trying to deal with some of their problems the people have given me much more than I could ever give them. I've learned much from them about their ability to cope with life despite poverty, illness, and tragedy. I learn from their ability to enjoy nature and live off the land, their ability to laugh at life with their never-ending tall tales and funny stories."

Under the leadership of Redeemer Pastor Dean Olson—"he's the real organizer," Chris claims—and Chris, a community literacy league has been formed. They meet at the public library and sponsor training for 40 tutors in the Laubach method of one-to-one teaching of reading. Now Chris is coordinating the effort of finding persons wanting to learn to read and matching them up with the tutors.

One of Chris's goals is to help her rural friends who are talented in some of the traditional Appalachian handicrafts to establish cooperative outlets for sale of their arts.

Wood carving is one of the arts. We drove through dogwood-covered hills to visit farmer Ed Cress who carves wildlife and domestic animals in all sizes from many kinds of wood. A wall full of ribbons attests to his skill. But Ed's a specialist—one of a handful in the United States—who carves larger-than-lifesize cigar store Indians. He's working on two of the big fellows now, one in the bedroom, one in the kitchen, both carved from buckeye.

"Oh, yes, they're still in demand," says Ed. "We can't keep up with the number folks want. But I've got to like a feller afore I'll carve him an Indian."

Quilting is probably the most popular Appalachian art. Just about every woman we visited had a quilt in a frame or tucked in the rafters to be finished when time allowed.

Chris thinks it's important to reinforce pride in the native art of quilting. She even started a quilting class, at first with members of the congregation, but now others come too. Mrs. Heninger was their first instructor.

"Members of the congregation have plugged into my ministry at several points," explained Chris. "When I learned of a family whose home had been destroyed by fire, one of our congregational families adopted them for Christmas, then went on to continue a rewarding relationship.

"Our women gave a kitchen shower for another family which had been burned out. The members of the congregation have really supported me in any ideas or projects I've proposed."

Chris is very sensitive about doing the kinds of ministry the church members and staff think she ought to be doing.

"Gee," she marvels. "I'm getting paid to do what a lot of people do voluntarily. I realize that it is the people in this church and in churches throughout the country who have made my work possible. It is a very sobering thought."

One of the churchly functions Chris performs dutifully but not delightedly is report making. Yet, even in reports Chris's high regard and loving concern for her mountain friends comes through. The report she dreaded most of all was the oral one she was asked to give at the synod convention.

But the delegates wouldn't have guessed her trepidation. They were so moved by the report—out of the many they had heard—that they gave Chris a standing ovation.

Every month Chris writes a folksy little report for the Redeemer newsletter. In one of them she told about the people: "They are my friends. They have given me more than I have given them. They send me on my way with treasures: arrowheads, home-canned vegetables, a bouquet of dogwood blossoms, a poke full of garden beans, some handmade flowers arranged in an empty potato chip can, a parcel of ham for my supper. They have given of themselves in sharing their lives with me."

I'm glad Chris is there to share. Thank God.

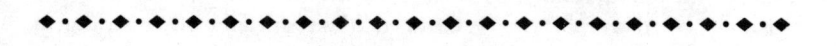

Sherrill Milnes:

Amazing Grace at the Met

by Thomas Orrin Bentz

A painted face peeks through the curtain fold into a spot of light to open *Pagliacci*. The Metropolitan Opera House is hushed. A clown leaps out, cavorts, kicks heels, claims his audience. He slips off the comic cap, sits—black hair shining in the near darkness—and sings. Rich baritones ring the silent tiers, touching other hearts and bringing down the house to sit beside him. Then he rises.

This is Sherrill Milnes. Here he stands, surrounded by red velvet and crystal chandeliers—a handsome, healthy, overnight star, already higher in this career than any of his lifetime dreams. On his fortieth birthday a full house of admirers sends down an avalanche of cheers.

After the opera, family, friends, and some of us fans carried on at his all-night birthday party. We bumped into stars and other strangers who dropped names and drank in the glamour. Yet the speeches were simple. There we mourned the sudden death of Richard Tucker and rejoiced in the successful life of Sherrill Milnes.

"This is a man who has not forgotten his roots," spoke Anderson Clark, arm upon Sherrill's shoulder. Anderson, a Presbyterian minister, is vice-president of Affiliate Artists Inc., a church-backed network of support for promising young musicians. Sherrill, a former Affiliate Artist, is taking time from his demanding schedule to serve as the new chairperson of their board of directors.

This is not a story of how to succeed in singing, or a portrait of an artist as a young man. It is a statement of faith, a story of soil and the soul.

"Bless the Lord, O my Soul," sings Sherrill Milnes on his RCA record album, *Amazing Grace*. The message is no accident. As surely as God chose us, Sherrill chose this music. It runs through his days and takes him back to the place where his faith flowered—on a farm outside Downers Grove, Illinois. It was recorded in the First Congregational United Church of Christ in downtown Downers Grove. "Bless the Lord" was composed by his cousin, Donald Drew, former organist at the church. The record is dedicated, like the church's organ that accompanies him, to his choir director and mother, Thelma Milnes.

Sherrill began in Indiana, where his father was pastor of a Methodist Church. "My first memory of church is sitting in the first pew with Mother. I look up and see Dad preaching. She looks down and sees my face. She licks her handkerchief and starts wiping my face. I make faces and start squirming. And she keeps scrubbing, taking away a layer of skin."

In 1940, James Milnes left the ministry for his personal health, perhaps also to save his son from being scrubbed to death before his eyes on Sunday mornings. Inheriting 300 acres of farmland from Thelma's father, C. K. Roe, they returned to Downers Grove.

"I had a calendar in my mind," Jim recalled. "But I didn't always take people along with me." He tried to start a cooperative farm with rural whites and city blacks, met with local resistance, then settled on the family land with Thelma, sons Roe and Sherrill, and some cows.

Though the cows have given way to horses, Jim is still there. Sherrill has him in mind when he sings of "The Old Rugged Cross."

Like his gritty dad, the triumphant son has a calendar in his mind. His calling takes people along with him. He has sung in Baltimore and Buenos Aires, from Chicago to Milan, even at the mecca of opera, the Staatsoper of Vienna. Everywhere the invitation is open again. Still Christmas finds him at home in Downers Grove, summer at his wife's family reunions in Iowa.

His mastered voice is heard on RCA Victor, London, and Angel records. Thirty years ago Sherrill sat in front of the Victrola and listened to old Victor recordings of Enrico Caruso. Each morning the Milnes family arose to the mellow tones of cows and the radio opera of Norman Ross.

Sherrill's first memory and influence in music was his mother—in a cameo of patience at the living room piano as a student pounded out a lesson. Sherrill played violin, but only when he had to. Some mornings he would slip downstairs and test his raspy, soprano vocal chords against a piano key to see if he had lowered a note overnight.

"He wanted to be a bass, but he sounded like a buzzsaw," said Mary Ann Humphreys, lifelong friend of the Mileses and mother of one of Thelma's piano prodigies. "Thelma used to say, 'Isn't it too bad. Sherrill will never be able to sing.'"

Nonsense. Whenever the Humphreys and Milneses got together, *everybody* played instruments and sang. Such a joyful noise soon overflowed the living room.

Thelma first directed her musical attention to the Presbyterian Church in town. Then in 1945, she claimed the choirs of First Congregational Church. Jim joined the basses. Sherrill, wide bow on white smock, went down the aisle with the boy's choir.

> A sparrow hath found . . . a house,
> and a swallow a nest
> where she may lay her young;
> even thine altars . . .
> O Lord of hosts, my king and my God!

"This church was Sherrill's second home; it has been the center of my life in this community," confessed Mary Ann, who headed its music committee when Thelma was director and now works in the day nursery school and family life program. "Thelma stood for a very high standard of music but she would not let it get in the way of people. It was always fun singing here. Sherrill still stops to see me when he gets home."

Last Christmas was his latest trip back to the low, snow-brushed moraines; to hardwood trees and home-made ice cream; to an ailing but bright-eyed father; to ninety-year-old aunts and thirty-year-old slide shows.

Screened transparencies frame the past in images that affirm the present. Family of four on the tractor ride to town for Christmas dinner. Rebuild a jalopy. Repair the roof. Practice piano, clarinet, horn, oboe, drums. Sing the "Messiah." Milk the cows. Run three miles to school. Model your own tattered maroon senior choir robe.

"Someone insisted that the setting of the *Amazing Grace* album cover, in front of the organ pipes in a choir robe, is just not me," Sherrill reflected. "Wrong. He just did not know me there. I've still sung more often in church than anyplace else."

Someone who did know him there is Edgar Cook, pastor of First Church for the last twenty-four years. "Sherrill's biography is a celebrity's dream: the farmboy makes it big. But he doesn't parade his past for publicity; his roots are real."

"His mother combined Christian dedication and top musicianship," continued Edgar, himself a trained musician. "She was 'dying' when I arrived here, but she battled cancer for twenty years and built an oratorio society that outgrew this church. When she died two days before their scheduled presentation of Mendelssohn's *Elijah*, Sherrill stepped in to conduct it in dedication to her."

When he came home to record *Amazing Grace* on her memorial organ, he dedicated "Calvary" to her father, Charlie Roe, road commissioner, lay preacher, and untrained country church soloist. Sherrill sang from his heart about the Easter promise.

Sherrill Milnes did not have a promising voice with his grandfather's natural gift; but he did have his mother's determination. "He was twenty percent voice, eighty percent development," remembered his pastor.

Edgar also recalled having an opinion snapped at by the star, who returned to conduct a concert in Downers Grove a few years ago. "When I told him I was hurt, he said, 'Edgar, I'm sorry. I didn't mean to disrespect you. You're still my pastor.'"

Then when Edgar suggested Sherrill sing three solos in First Church last Christmas, he was reminded of a different disrespect. "No, this is not a concert," warned the big baritone. "We are here to worship God."

Let us praise God
together on our knees . . .

"Going to church meant doing something I loved—singing," said the vocalist who advanced to his mother's adult choir as a grade-school tenor. "I also loved high school; I had a few subjects in between music. I had a violin and a tinny voice, but I was too big to be called a sissy.

"I played football one year and ran cross-country another, but the farm work was too much," added the sturdy six-footer, one of three farm kids in a school of a thousand students. "If rain was coming tomorrow, and you had thirty acres of baled hay out in the field when the sun went down, you went on working through midnight until you got it all into the hay mow.

"Solidarity, soil, roots, family strength—here is where the church has got to serve," he summarized. "People split off too soon. Keep the roots. Old folks and young folks can live together."

One day, after two decades of song in the fields outside Downers Grove, Sherrill was called from the barn to the phone. Someone wanted a hefty, masculine sound for a commercial. "If they could have seen me—pitchfork, bib-overalls, and workshoes," he chuckled, "they would have hung up. I really looked hayseed and tacky."

Yet unseen, he sounded his way into our minds, and throats with the jingle of a popular beer commercial. Then he rode the theme from "The Magnificent Seven" out into horse country and turned his popular voice on the Marlboro song.

He got a lot to like from Marlboro, enough to buy new blue robes for the First Church choir. After 18 years of Sunday mornings in the choir loft and a career-launching repertoire of religious music, this was Sherrill Milnes' way to say thank you. So is *Amazing Grace* a tribute: to the God who gave him a song; to the parents who showed him how to sing it; to all the faithful who would sing along.

"You've got to start where you are," stated Jim Milnes. "I came to this land broke. I believe I should share it. This country is dedicated to the almighty dollar, everybody for self. We've got to cooperate and give more." He has given most of what he had to the YMCA, the church, the Evangelical Hospital Association, and now lives on seven acres. "I love producing something, watching a plant come up. Our boys learned where their food, their lives, came from."

"I want to show the music I grew up on and my feeling about it," said Sherrill, sharing the hymns and songs on *Amazing Grace* and *The Church's One Foundation,* another recent release. "They are part of what I am. Everything I did on these recordings is corny, basic, gut reaction. Music is primarily emotional, secondarily intellectual. I have grown immune to the so-called sophisticates."

"This music hasn't been recorded much. It isn't Bach or Beethoven," the artist admitted. "But I think that Bach and Beethoven would have loved this stuff."

"This is worthy, beautiful music," he added, as if embracing the efforts of all church choirs everywhere. "It deserves your best effort; don't slough it off. You need variety in music; do some experimenting. But do come back to the old hymns."

Successful master of his own vocal chords, near consummate artist in mid-career, Sherrill Milnes comes back. Singing arias on a tractor, he still has an earthy ease about himself, gathered in a steady harvest of family, friends, and faith.

Raymon B. Fogg:

Hope After the Hurricane

by Marilynne Hill

A minister's morning prayer doesn't always bear such dramatic fruit as one did on a Sunday morning in Cleveland, Ohio, when Terry J. Van Heyningen, pastor of the North Royalton Christian Church, prayed for the victims of Hurricane Fifi. The prayer was answered through a member of his congregation.

Raymon B. Fogg, engineer and contractor, is a pilot who owns a plane. He wondered if the plane could be used to help in relief efforts. Through his denomination's national office, he offered his services for "up to thirty days" to Church World Service.

The hurricane struck the last week in September, 1974, devastating the tiny Central American republic of Honduras. By October 4, Mr. Fogg was on his way to Honduras with a thousand-pound load of food. When he arrived, it was raining and too late to do more than unload. A military guard was mounted over supplies to prevent looting. Some eager and not very responsible reporter saw the guard and assumed that the local military had confiscated the relief supplies. Later, when Mr. Fogg read the news item released by this reporter, he was furious.

For several days he worked with others delivering relief supplies—by plane if he could, by jeepload where planes couldn't land, and on foot and carrying 100-pound sacks of grain on his shoulder in places where jeeps could not travel.

Some ill-informed but probably well-meaning donor had sent a load of canned sauerkraut which, like the guard mounted by the military, was the source of some misinterpretation in the press. Relief workers recognized the fact that sauerkraut was practically unknown to the Hondurans, and in any case, the Honduran economy is not based on the use of can openers. The canned sauerkraut was sold to people who would eat it, and the proceeds used for beans which the Hondurans needed.

Church World Service was asked by the World Council of Churches to act as coordinator for relief efforts in Honduras. The ecumenical Protestant agency in Honduras is CEDEN, and CEDEN was the agency CWS worked through in this emergency.

The damage was not done by the wind; the hurricane stalled just off the coast. But the clouds dumped their excessively heavy rain accumulation in the mountains. Huge walls of water carried sand, gravel, boulders, houses, cattle, uprooted trees and crops down the valleys. Devastation was complete. Between 8,000 and 10,000 persons were killed and 300,000 to 350,000 persons were homeless. Food and shelter were the immediate critical needs.

As the CWS workers observed the devastation they began to wonder what the people would eat when the relief food was gone. More than half the country's agricultural production was lost; eighty percent of the banana crop was washed away, with tools and seeds. They listed what a family would need to replace its flooded-out crops.

Several times Mr. Fogg loaded his plane with tents before he began to think of something more permanent. Then he looked around, observing the kind of houses the people of Honduras lived in. He sent for Ralph Tacker, a friend in the construction business back home, and soon the two of them were working out a technique for building tilt-up walls. Using sand and gravel washed down by the flood, they cast concrete slabs, which were then hoisted into position. Using this technique, they built concrete houses with concrete floor, metal roof, doors, and windows—for about $360 each. The building process was organized into a series of operations to be done, production-line fashion, by four or five men. Using this system, they built four houses a day. Before Mr. Fogg returned to Cleveland in November, he had work crews raising houses in three different locations, and three more locations had been projected.

From the beginning, as Mr. Fogg worked with the people, helping them to build their houses, he said to the men as they worked together, "As soon as you have finished building your homes, you must begin to erect your house of worship. You need a church." A year later the church was under construction.

One day he noticed two boys loading gravel into a wheelbarrow. One pushed the wheelbarrow while the other, with a rope around his waist, pulled. Together they were doing a man's work. Both boys, about eleven years old, were the only surviving members of their families. Mr. Fogg asked if they didn't want to go to the city where he was sure he could find a home for them. The boys looked at each other. Then the spokesman said, "If our fathers were alive, they'd be helping to build the houses of our friends. We'll stay as long as we can help."

When Mr. Fogg returned to Cleveland in November, he began telling people, "For $15 we can buy in Honduras what a family needs to ensure a harvest." The packets contained—besides the tools—some seeds, a cooking pot, a frying pan, a grinder for corn, and a plate, cup and spoon for each member of the family.

The construction work had struck a snag. A heavy crane was needed for lifting the concrete wall slabs into position. Mr. Fogg designed a wooden hoist which could be made of trees uprooted or damaged by boulders, but he worried about its safety. In Cleveland, he constructed a safe hoist and arranged for shipping it to Honduras.

The construction workers needed a truck. Mr. Fogg knew where he could get one and, he thought, a driver who would take it to Honduras loaded with supplies. Church World Service paid for the truck, but the driver backed out at the last minute. Mr. Fogg flew to San Antonio, saw to the loading, and set out. He ate his Thanksgiving dinner, cold baked beans and crackers, sitting on some Mayan ruins somewhere in Central America.

The night before Mr. Fogg left for Cleveland, one of the Hondurans said to him, "How can you leave us? You are our *esperanza*." His interpreter translated that as, "You are our hope."

This expression of trust and appreciation touched Mr. Fogg, and he found himself planning to return as soon as possible, to spend more time in Honduras.

Literally hundreds of congregations in the Midwest have heard him tell his story, enriched by colorful slides and recorded music from Honduras. Responding to him and his concern, many North Americans have learned to share the suffering of another people in a way they never experienced before.

Asked by one interviewer why he went to Honduras, Mr. Fogg replied, "I'm no mystic, but I think God speaks to you very clearly sometimes, telling you to respond to certain needs. I believe He told me to go to Honduras."

"The Lady":

She Reached Out with Love

by Jean D. Ketchum

Several years ago, I had reached an "all-time low." Due to various events which seemed very traumatic to me, I could see little point in carrying on with this thing called life. In my ever-growing self-pity, I began caring less and less about anything or anyone, even the people I loved most.

The day began just as all the rest had begun in the past couple of months. It was cold and snowing as I left for work, but I really didn't care about that, or anything else. After the thirty-minute routine drive, I climbed the stairs of the insurance company for which I worked, and headed toward my office. As always, I passed several other employees and said my usual "Good Morning."

One of the people I passed was a woman named Elizabeth, who worked in another department. I had never really given her much thought, but had decided long before that she was very classy and proper, and had dubbed her "The Lady." At that time, I used the term not only to make fun of her perfect composure, but also with a tinge of envy because I didn't have it. I often noticed that nothing ruffled her, nothing angered her, and nothing could make that perpetual smile disappear from her face. That type of "goodie" tended to frighten me, so I avoided her like the plague. I was polite and friendly, but there I drew the line.

That afternoon, I was feeling particularly bad about my situation in general, and the thought of working was far from my mind. The Lady worked in a department directly across from mine, and her desk was situated so that when I looked out the window of my office, she was the first person I saw. I glanced up after a telephone call and was ready to go for coffee when all of a sudden that face of hers came into view. The people around her seemed to fade to the background and she had a glow like I've never seen in my life. I sat and stared at her for what must have seemed to her an eternity. I couldn't imagine what in the world was happening, but I couldn't take my eyes off her.

I wondered about that experience for several days, and seemed to find myself looking at that Lady more and more and all the time, wondering what it was she had that made her stand out. I first decided she was a phony and set out to prove it. I began to talk to her every time I had the chance and began to find situations where I could be alone with her so that we could really have some discussions. I began to realize that "religion," "God," and "Christ" seemed to be an integral part of her philosophy and her life-style, and that these words were used a great deal in most all our conversations. I had had a religious background, but somehow, for me, it didn't take. To me, a "church-goer" was a "church-goer," and that was about all there was to it. I believed in God, and knew He was up there doing something, but was much too busy to be bothered with me. I figured I had to make my own way, and that when things went wrong, I'd have to work them out by myself.

I became very confused. I had set out to prove to myself that The Lady was a phony, and as time went by I was becoming more and more convinced that *she* was for real and *I* was the phony. Even after I knew that was the way it was, I still couldn't help wondering how anyone could possibly feel the way she does. How does one care so much about everyone else, and find the good in everyone else, and not be frightened of what tomorrow might bring? I still couldn't figure her out. All I knew was that The Lady was really beginning to grow on me; and I felt she liked me, too, even though I thought I could sometimes see a little of the frustration she must have felt in trying to get through to me.

I began to write little notes to her, usually on the humorous side, and much to my surprise, she wrote back. Many times, her replies included something about religion. The Lady became more and more of an enigma and more and more of a challenge. In my effort to destroy an image, I found the most genuinely beautiful human being I had ever known. I then proceeded to put her on a pedestal so high she was completely beyond my reach. I knew it and so did she, and I think it was at this point she decided to sit back and let God try to figure me out.

Without really knowing why, I began to give religion a great deal of thought, and even began going to church on a regular basis again. I was searching for that wonderful thing that made The Lady able to face each situation with courage and strength. During this period, I spent a great deal of time with her and asked many questions. She must have wondered if it would *ever* sink in!

Fortunately, because of her stamina and a wonderful minister, it all became clear. As lightening strikes, Christ came into the picture, and I knew I never had to face another situation alone, never had to be afraid of life, and never had to make my own way again. I know God used that wonderful Lady in order to find me, and for that, and the rare friendship she and I have developed, I thank Him many times each day.

Now, as I look at that face I've grown to love so much, I can't help thinking how marvelous it would be if we would all allow God to work through us as she does. We all must be prepared and must search for that part of us which God can use to reach others. Each day, we find the opportunity and the struggling souls, crying out for help. Many times, those cries must be heard through a veil of jealousy, anger and even hatred. I thank God that The Lady looked beyond that veil to the great need within, reflecting a form of the love for one another that He intended for us all.

Testimony of Hope:

He Makes Today Count

by Orville E. Kelly

This year a million Americans will discover that they have cancer. Many other millions will continue to lead unhappy lives, to do things they do not really want to do, and to worry about death. We all seem to be running to keep up with the flow of technological advances and with our jobs.

We're placed upon this earth at birth, and we die. Between those times we can do nothing about the past. But if we're unhappy, we can certainly do something about the future.

We all seem to be afraid to lose the material things we've accumulated on earth and afraid to face the fact that there's more to life than birth.

There is death. This is a part of life. We're so concerned about life after death that we forget how to live the lives that we have here on earth. It escapes us somehow. And we just cannot contend with the thought that someday the sun will come up, the world will go on and we won't be here.

With me, I guess I could say that life ended at forty-two when I discovered I had cancer. It began again at forty-three when I readjusted my life.

Once I discovered I had cancer and went through the extensive tests and weeks in hospitals, I was depressed. As time went on, I was afraid. They didn't suddenly walk in and say, "Hey, you're going to die." Instead they gave me statistics, diagnosed my disease as lymphoma, told me where the cancer was located in my body.

So one day I just asked the doctor, "Am I going to die of cancer?"

He said, "Yes, unless something else kills you first."

(A man I grew up with told me a while back, "You know, it's really terrible that you have cancer." I felt it was, too. About three months ago he died of a heart attack.)

Nevertheless, I was in a period of depression. Why me, God? I wondered; there are worse people around. I even thought about killing myself.

People were ill at ease around me. My family was falling apart. My wife was under a doctor's care for a nervous condition because of me. My children were failing in school. My own relatives didn't want to be around me. I didn't want to be around anyone else.

I wanted to identify with someone, but I didn't know who. The physicians were treating my body for cancer. The ministers were talking to me about the hereafter. But nobody could tell me how to straighten out my mind.

One sunny autumn day I was driving back from a chemotherapy treatment in Iowa City. Beautiful fields stretched out ahead of me, and just for a moment I forgot about the cancer.

Then I looked over at my wife beside me. I can't describe her look of sorrow and despair. It suddenly struck me how everything was falling apart because of me.

I wasn't dead yet; I wasn't ready to die yet; I wasn't going to die yet. In fact I felt pretty good that day. But I had been creating my own hell on earth.

So I turned to my wife and said, "Wanda, let's talk about it." We had never really discussed my cancer or the fact that I was dying. "Let's go home and tell the children. But then let's have some fun. Let's barbecue tonight."

Since then I'm happy again. We still have our problems. I still wake up in the morning sometimes and think it's all a bad dream. Then I go downstairs and see the sun break across the horizon—not another day closer to death, but another day of life with which I am blessed.

Once I had decided to try to make each day count, I felt it could work for others. I wrote a story in the local paper calling terminally ill persons to come together with their families to work out their problems. This is how Make Today Count started. Now it is a national organization with membership open to terminally ill patients and their families. Physicians, nurses and others concerned about the terminally ill may be associate members.

We had eighteen people at the first meeting. I told them: "We're not here tonight to discuss who has the worst case of cancer or who is going to die first. We're here to organize a group to learn how to live each day as fully and completely as we can."

Since then, I initiated letter writing and home visitation programs to terminally ill persons who cannot attend meetings, and Make Today Count chapters have started in cities across the country.

I have good memories of my life. I've been in Paris in the springtime to walk along the bridges of the Seine, and on an island in the South Pacific to watch days of blazing sunshine across a blue lagoon. I've been to Oktoberfest in Germany, and to Tokyo on a misty summer evening.

But I have lived more in the past few months than I lived in all the years of my preceding life because now I'm aware of life itself. Now a Saturday night candelight supper with my wife in our kitchen after we've put the kids to bed is greater—awaking each morning is greater—than walking the bridges of the Seine.

I do not count time anymore as it flows by, as many people record it on a calendar. I measure time, perhaps, in the moment it takes to see my wife smile or my children run by my window and not be sad but glad.

I made a lot of promises to my children as they were growing up that I never had time to keep. Last fall I took them to the woods; I had never done that before. This year I will see the earth flower as I have never done before, and I will take time to touch the heartstrings of someone in need.

A young executive called me and said, "I'm making money. I have a wife, a five-year-old son, and a new car. We're all healthy but I'm unhappy. So how can you be happy when you're dying?"

I said, "Tonight when you get home, go into your son's bedroom, look at his face and if you feel like it, reach down and give him a kiss. Then go and have a conversation with your wife. Walk out in your yard, look up at the stars and pray for just a little bit. Think what you want out of life, what you want to do and thank God for what you have. Then perhaps happiness as you call it may begin to find you."

A young woman phoned and said, "Please call my father; he's dying." So I did. When he answered I said, "I guess we have something in common." He said, "Yes, we're both dying of cancer." I answered, "No; we're both still alive." I don't consider myself dying of cancer, but learning to live with it.

Don't be afraid to die; don't be afraid to live. Do what you want to do. Pay for your mistakes, then start over again.

I am often asked, "How can you believe in God? You can't see him or touch him." Well, I love my wife and children very deeply, but I can't reach out and put my hand on that love. I can feel a breeze brush my cheek, but I can't reach out and hold it in my hand. That's the way I feel about God; I feel his presence all around me.

I ask you to join me tomorrow morning in welcoming a new day and trying your best to make it count. Don't take it for granted. It is a gift to you. For now, let me give you a prayer that I once wrote when sleep came a little hard:

Heavenly Father, give me the strength to face each night before the dawn. Give me the courage to watch my children at play and my wife at my side without a trace of sorrow in my smile. Let me count each passing moment as I once marked the fleeting days and months. Give me hope for each tomorrow and let my dreams be of the future. When life here on earth is over, let there be no sadness, but only joy for the golden days I have had. Amen.

Mr. Smith of Brown Creek:

Teaching Lessons to the Preacher

by William H. Willimon

The small brick structure stood amidst an expansive, unkempt cemetery, and tried to look dignified, even though the sign out front was peeling and leaning to one side.

Brown Creek, the oldest congregation in the county, at one time had been prosperous. Now the congregation consisted of a handful of older people who had been farmers and a few of their children who commuted to factory jobs in Atlanta. In its recent struggle for existence, it had been served by a yearly succession of reluctant student pastors.

"Let's face it," said the lay leader, Mr. Smith, who met my wife, Patsy, and me that first afternoon, "without that graveyard, there wouldn't be no church here. Folks is here 'cause their kin is out there." He gestured to the irregular rows of tombstones by the church.

"Once a year we have a crowd for the Moore-Bridewell Reunion. We have a guest preacher and a big dinner out under them pine trees. You can guess why they come here every year?"

"The graveyard?" I ventured, knowing I was all too correct.

Mr. Smith was to be my confidant, my mentor, my strongest advocate during my pastorate at Brown Creek Church (and cemetery). He was an amazing person. Although he had only a fourth-grade education, he had, with great native ability, built a prosperous construction company. He let me have one Sunday on my own. Then probably noting my woeful lack of ability, he tactfully took me aside and gave me my first lesson on how to be a successful preacher.

"You see that we are just country people. We like good preachin'. You'll need to be a good preacher if you're going to make it here."

I asked him to be specific.

"Well, we don't go for no educated preacher. The quicker you forget that stuff you learned in seminary, the better they'll like you. And don't never use no notes when you preach. We like a man to get his sermons fresh, straight from the Lord. And move around a lot when you're preaching. Shout if you feel like it. They love that. They like to see a preacher with some fire in him."

"Should I wear a robe when I preach?" I asked, knowing even as I asked what the answer would be.

"Lord, no!" replied Mr. Smith. "They'll think you're a Catholic!"

He laughed and I laughed, but down inside I was wondering if my tenure at Brown Creek was going to be a laughing matter. I had just graduated from Yale Divinity School in New Haven, Connecticut, and my wife had finished her master's degree. We had come down South for a year of graduate work at Emory University in Atlanta before we returned home to South Carolina and to full-time ministry.

And so the next Sunday I cast my notes aside, gesticulated, and shouted. Except for three full-throated infants who protested during the entire service, the people seemed pleased.

We had no choir at Brown Creek, but the people loved to sing the old gospel songs. These were printed in little brown hymnals with shaped notes, a system of musical notation devised by an evangelist many years ago for country churches where few people had formal musical training. The pianist (Mr. Smith's wife, Opal) played with great spirit even though her only piano lessons were obtained through a correspondence course. We sang hymns I had never heard of; lively, toe-tapping tunes of questionable theological content: *The Royal Telephone* ("You can always ring up Jesus / the line is never busy") and *The Eastern Gate.*

My wife found an undiscovered talent for singing when Mr. Smith talked her into singing duets with him. Everybody's favorite was their rendition of *How Great Thou Art,* with modifications in the tune each time they sang it.

"Patsy hit one of the highest notes ever hit in this church," complimented one lady on the way out of church one morning.

Mr. Smith immediately spoke up. "That's natural. She and Will has been to college, you know."

Not everyone was pleased with me as their new pastor. The song leader, Brother Joe, was cold to me from the day of our first meeting. In country churches the song leader is an important person. He directs the worship service, selects and leads the hymn singing, recognizes visitors and those members who have had recent birthdays. The minister's main responsibilities in worship are preaching and praying.

I had nothing against Brother Joe, but I did get a little uncomfortable hearing his often repeated petition to the Lord to "spare this church from the decay of recent years."

One evening, after I had been at Brown Creek for a few months, Brother Joe informed me that "the Lord has led me into greener fields of service" and that he would not be with us any longer. I said that I hoped my coming had nothing to do with his going.

"Well, as a matter of fact, you are the main reason," admitted Brother Joe.

Mr. Smith, conscious of my hurt feelings at losing a member, now assumed the role of song leader along with his other responsibilities as chairman of our church board, custodian, trustee of the cemetery, and chairman of the Moore-Bridewell Reunion Committee.

Mr. Smith was not only the biggest financial contributor among our twenty-five or so members but he was my most staunch defender. He had decided that the church needed an "educated preacher like they have in Atlanta" and he seemed pleased with my qualifications.

He told me one Sunday that a preacher from another denomination "was jumpin' on you yesterday at the gas station."

"Me?" I asked.

"Yeah. He was sayin' that Brown Creek had gone to the devil. Said we had a Yankee out here preachin' for us. An atheist. Said if we had any religion or guts, we would run you off. I told him he was crazy, that you was from South Carolina."

Some attitudes surprised me. Having served a conservative, wealthy, upper-class congregation while at school in Connecticut, I was unprepared for the outlook of my people at Brown Creek toward some of the pressing issues of the day. They were uniformly against the war in Vietnam (this was 1970-71). Their sons and relatives were doing most of the fighting and dying, and their attitude was, "What has them people way over there done to us?"

They had an inherent distrust for the federal government. Most supported socialized medicine, having been victimized again and again by the inequities of our present health-care system. One couple with a combined income of $6,500 a year owed $7,000 for an operation by a doctor who owned a chain of motels.

In a region long known for its racism, my little congregation displayed less hostility toward black people than the people I had worked with in Connecticut. They knew what it means to be locked out of the system. Most of them worked each day alongside black men and women. A union service we had on Thanksgiving with a black church revealed the down-to-earth, genuine regard my people felt for their black neighbors.

Like every minister, I had good Sundays and bad Sundays. It was frustrating to drive the 30 miles from Atlanta on a rainy Sunday evening to find only two members (usually Mr. and Mrs. Smith) in attendance.

Lack of money was a perennial problem. Mr. Smith dutifully paid me my salary, $200 each month, though I am sure he had to pad the monthly offering to provide the full amount.

"Country folks loves the Lord," he commented, "but, like city folks, they loves their money more."

Formerly, he said, ministers were expected to exist on their parishioners' extra vegetables and sporadic "love offerings." "Lots of folks think that when you start payin' a preacher, he'll get soft," Mr. Smith explained.

I noted, however, that proportionally more of our offering went to missions than was given at most larger churches I had known. People at

Brown Creek had the firm conviction that "with the world in such a mess, we ought to do all we can for it."

In addition to visiting the sick, Mr. Smith and I made a valiant effort to encourage backsliders to return to church. Admittedly, this was not my favorite chore since I got the impression that our visits were not welcomed. Naturally, we were met by a host of excuses listing a variety of strange maladies. One person got "nervous in crowds" (crowds at Brown Creek?) and one man said there was a strange odor in our sanctuary that made him sneeze.

"Them folks needs a good kick in the rear more than a preacher," Mr. Smith commented.

When I led Bible study on Sunday evening, the small group of faithful seemed to enter into these sessions with much seriousness—as long as I ended in time for everyone to get home to watch *Bonanza* on TV.

As I had been told, the highlight of the year was the annual Moore-Bridewell Reunion. Here was a time for seeing old friends again, filling the church to capacity, and having a gigantic meal out under the pine trees beside the cemetery.

Brother Bob Rogers, a local plumber and relative of the Bridewells', was to be the guest preacher. He seemed to be a pleasant, rather mild-mannered fellow, but viewed me with a bit of distrust, especially when he learned that I was a seminary graduate.

Brother Bob's sermon was like nothing I have ever heard before. He started out in rather mild tones, dwelling on the significance of Ezekiel's biblical references to oxen and wheels and fire, recalling his days as a farmer and how difficult it was to plow with stubborn mules and how much he would have appreciated having had an ox to use. A few people said "Amen" at this remark. Then Brother Bob removed his coat and tie, leaned over the pulpit, and rolled up each shirt sleeve as if to signal that he was getting down to business.

The sermon got louder and louder as he touched on everything from the sinfulness of the Vietnam War to the waywardness among the rich people in Atlanta. Tears came to his eyes when he thought of all the good Christian Bridewells buried out in the graveyard, and his face grew redder and redder until I feared for his health. He flailed and shouted, snorted and fumed. Then, when it was over, we sang a hymn and went out to eat dinner under the pines.

Mr. Smith must have sensed some of my discomfort during the sermon, for he took me aside that afternoon.

"You know, some of us have been talking. We got to comparing your sermons and Bob's."

I began to fear that I wouldn't come out too well.

"Now, Bob, he's a good man. But he ain't got no education. That kind of preachin' used to be all there was. But we like the way you preach. You give us something to think about. Something to take home. We want you to be the preacher next year at the Moore-Bridewell Reunion, if you're still with us."

I was touched by their vote of confidence, for they had bestowed upon me their highest honor.

"Yes," remarked Mr. Smith as I headed to my car for the return trip to Atlanta, "a few years ago I wouldn't have given a damn for a preacher that preached the whole sermon with his coat and tie on. But times change, don't they?"

Yes, times change. And time moves on. I moved on that June. Having finished my graduate studies, I was ready to return to South Carolina to take up some new Brown Creek Church. The people at Brown Creek had a farewell dinner for us out on the grounds, under the pine trees by the graveyard. There were tears and some good memories.

I suppose that the people of Brown Creek are a passing phenomenon. Progress, a strange thing that comes out of places like Atlanta, is sweeping them away. The people of Brown Creek were poor, they were exasperating, they were wonderful. They were people very much like the people who followed Jesus around Nazareth. And the people at Brown Creek Church taught me that year, in some measure, why he loved people like them so much.

Uncle Gus:

Legacy of a Last Reunion

by Jack Moore

Mister John Henry Bishop and his good wife, Miz Nora Fleeta Faulkner Bishop, were the parents of 12 children. Then they raised and called their own, one more. Not counting grandchildren.

If I ever could, I am no longer able to fit them in the correct chronological order. Took me a spell to remember all the names. In any order.

First was my mother, Lilla. Not that she was the oldest, but just first. For me and Nell and Nolie, her children.

Then there were Sam and Ollie, Quintus and Tookie, Lera and Josie Lee, Claiborne and Ellen, and Annie Laurie.

And Uncle Gus, who died just a few weeks ago.

Leaving only two of the 13. Genevieve and Ruby.

One of my Mississippi cousins called to tell me about Uncle Gus. To say that he had asked that his nephews be the pallbearers.

There are not many of us left, he said. We know it's a long way and everything, and it's asking a lot, but will you come?

I wonder?

If anyone of us really knows how far it is? From one lifetime to another? Who can measure the distance traveled in eighteen years away from your homeland? Or in eighteen months, for that matter?

I went.

And I sure am glad.

My Uncle Gus was a right smart man. Remembered with love and fondness by hundreds, maybe thousands, for his activities as a school teacher. Long since retired, he spent the last decade or so scrounging good reading materials for country schools. Where mostly the students are black. And nearly all of them poor.

I don't think he really cared who carried his casket. I really don't. He wasn't the kind of man to set much store on something like that.

But he was a great lover of family reunions. And he wanted us to have one. A last one with him.

He wanted the children of his beloved family to gather and renew the bonds that have been frayed by distance and time. To talk about our children and their children. And be drawn closer, if only for a little while.

To share once again the oft-told stories of the escapades of the Bishop boys and the pranks of the Bishop girls. To laugh and to cry and to celebrate the memories. And all they mean.

A precious part of our heritage.

Don't know what sort of an estate my Uncle Gus left. Probably not much in material things. School teachers rarely get rich.

But he left me a lot of warm and cheerful reminders of the family love that cherished and nurtured me in the days when my roots were green. And fragile.

And the legacy of his last reunion. For now.

He left me with a new insight.

The distance is not so great as it was. And never so great as we think.
O God, thank you for gifts little recognized, for turning back the covers of hidden understanding, for tearing down the barriers of life's realities, and equipping us to grasp the hope of your tomorrows. Amen.

Feeding the Hungry:

She Heard God Say "GO!"

by Kathryn Waller

> Kathryn Waller spearheaded a volunteer outreach program to increase the number of persons in Charlotte, North Carolina, who receive food stamps. During the period of the program, the total number of these persons (including children) increased from 15,000 to 41,000. Following is Mrs. Waller's personal narrative of the experience, given as part of a conference on world and domestic hunger held in Atlanta, Georgia.

And it came to pass that one day the Lord spoke to Kathryn as she was happily working in her garden:
"Kathryn, why do you mock me?"
And Kathryn said, "Lord, I don't know what you're talking about. I never meant to mock you."
And the Lord responded, "Every time you pray to me, every time you beat your breast and cry aloud to me for my children who are hungry, you mock me. Did I not give you an able body and an adequate mind? Have I not comforted you, strengthened you, and in every way nourished you and protected you since the day you were born?"
And she said, "Yes, Lord."
And He spoke again, saying, "Why then do you pretend to care for these my children when you waste your time on everything under the sun, but for the hungry you lift not a finger?"
Then Kathryn was moved to anger, saying, "That's not true, Lord. Haven't I given my tithe to the church? Haven't I slaved over a hot church stove once a week, cooking meals for the poor? Haven't I carried baskets of food to the destitute and even, from time to time, shared my home with the homeless? Others have done far less. Why are you picking on me?"
But God was not moved, and He said, "If you love my children, then help them to feed themselves. Give them the means to provide for their families. Find a way to make a permanent difference in their lives. I'm sick of your Band-Aids and your sometime charity. Use the mind and body I gave you. Look around you in Charlotte, North Carolina, and set my people free from hunger."
So Kathryn left her garden and pondered what she should do and how she should begin. And it happened that when she was meeting one night with her community, The Community of the Fellowship of Jesus, she said, "I am going to try to do something about the problem of hunger. Who will help me?"
And straightway, fifteen people said to her, "You lead; we'll follow."
Now there was at the same time a man named Dr. Raymond Wheeler abiding in that town. Dr. Wheeler was a man of great wisdom concerning hunger for he had served on a Senate committee that probed the cause and extent of hunger in the United States. So Kathryn sought his counsel.
And he said, "The government has decreed that all the people should have enough to eat, and this decree is called the Food Stamp Program. But the Food Stamp Program doesn't reach even a third of the poor

people in North Carolina or many more, for that matter, in the U.S. Go find out why it doesn't work and make it work. Then go to Washington and tell the government what you learned so it can correct its mistakes."

And Kathryn was sore troubled for she did not know how to do this thing.

And then it came to pass that God called the Charlotte Area Fund to form a hunger task force, and Kathryn was exceedingly glad for she and her people could work together with the task force to make this thing that Dr. Wheeler had spoken of come to pass.

So the Community Hunger Task Force and the Charlotte Area Fund Hunger Task Force joined hands, and together they set forth to find the poor and hungry people of Charlotte and Mecklenburg County in order to tell them of the Food Stamp Program and to help them become certified for food stamps so they could feed themselves and their families—not just a meal here and there but three meals a day, seven days a week.

And when the job was done, Kathryn went back to her garden, feeling happy and content.

But it happened that God found her there one morning and said, "Kathryn, I want you to go to Chapel Hill. Go to a hunger conference there and tell the people what has come to pass in Charlotte."

And Kathryn said, "No way, Lord! You know I don't make speeches. Why do you ask me to do something you know I can't do? Even Moses you didn't force to make a speech but instead sent his brother Aaron to speak for him. Send someone else to Chapel Hill."

But God would not listen to her and only said in a louder voice, "Go to Chapel Hill."

And again Kathryn was moved to anger, and she said, "Haven't I worked for one solid year for you? Haven't I attended more than 100 neighborhood meetings, informing and assisting the poor in their search for food stamps? Haven't I looked them in the face, agonized over their heavy labor and low wages, their aching backs and proud hearts, their little children with eyes full of hopes and dreams?

"Haven't I met with county commissioners and others in authority to help them see the need to make the program work? And haven't I earned the right to putter around in my garden now that 20,000 more people in Charlotte and Mecklenburg County are being fed, who previously were hungry?"

But God was not moved, and He said, "GO!"

So Kathryn went in fear and trembling, to Chapel Hill. And there God caused her to learn that 600,000 of his children in North Carolina were hungry and did not know where to turn or to whom they could cry for help.

So Kathryn went home to Charlotte and told her community's hunger task force of all she had learned in Chapel Hill, and together they decided to go into all of North Carolina, county by county, telling the concerned and compassionate people in every county of the plight of the poor and the means they could use to alleviate hunger.

And so it was that they began to write to hundreds of God's people, and some were called Episcopalians, and others were called Presbyterians, and still others were called Roman Catholics and Methodists. And to each of these they offered to come and teach and train volunteers to go out in their own counties and make the Food Stamp Program reach the hungry.

Then it was that Kathryn's heart began to grow heavy for some of God's people wrote back and said, "Come and talk to us, and we will see what we will do."

But others wrote back and said, "Do not come for we are busy studying."

And another said, "Do not come for our people are busy fasting."

And another said, "Do not come for we have sent our money to the Presiding Bishop's Fund for World Relief."

And another said, "We do not like government money."

And another said, "We are having a garden tour to raise money."

And another said, "We are writing a cookbook."

And another said, "We do not want to become personally involved; we just want to give money."

And another said, "If they weren't lazy, they wouldn't be hungry."

And another said, "If we feed them, they won't work."

And another said, "Let them eat red tape."

And most said nothing at all.

So Kathryn sought out God and cried aloud, saying, "Lord, what can I do? If the people in your churches won't help me, to whom can I turn for help?"

And God said, "Have I not led you every step of the way? Why do you doubt me? I will show you a way. Yet a little while longer will I wait on my churches to cease their endless talk and act to feed my children. It is not for you to question me, only to stop when I say 'Stop' and go when I say 'Go.' The cries of the poor are loud in my ears, and my heart is sorely moved. Be still, and I will show you and others who care how to help my children feed themselves."

And so it was that Kathryn saw her work was not yet finished. She kept all these things and pondered them in her heart.

Alex Gilmore:

Making Friends for the Church

by James Taylor

When Alex Gilmore was first elected a United Church elder, he went to call on his congregation's Sunday school superintendent. As he walked along the sidewalk, he passed a couple of young men visiting door-to-door for the Seventh Day Adventists. Then he met a couple of Jehovah's Witnesses coming down the front steps. When he knocked on the door, it opened a few inches only.

A woman said: "I've had enough church for one night," and slammed the door.

"Fortunately," Gilmore recalls, "her husband recognized my voice, and quickly reopened the door as I turned to leave. So then she insisted I stay for tea."

It was the beginning of many happy experiences as a visiting elder. He was forty-three years old before he was elected to the session of his church, North Lonsdale United, North Vancouver, British Columbia. (He has since been an elder at three other B.C. churches.) But even before his election he already had had a great deal of church experience. In 1923, at age nineteen, he served on a committee that united the Presbyterian and Methodist churches in Steveston, on the Fraser River. He was a delegate to the service of inauguration of The United Church of Canada, June 10, 1925, at what was then St. Andrew's Presbyterian Church in Vancouver.

But the real joy of his church associations, now that Alex Gilmore has turned seventy and looks back, was being an elder.

He recalls visiting, on a survey, an elderly Norwegian widower who didn't want to see anyone from any church. "I was raised a Lutheran," he told Mr. Gilmore, "in a church so strict you had to get the preacher's permission to sneeze." At least, that's a polite version of what he said. Taking a guess, based on the vigor and content of the man's language, Mr. Gilmore asked if he might happen to be a commercial fisherman.

"You're *%$+* right I am," came the answer.

"I'm in the fishing business, too," said Mr. Gilmore.

"I know all about that *%$+* fishers of men stuff," came the reply. But after Mr. Gilmore convinced him that he was, in fact, production manager for a fishing company, the Norwegian's tune changed. "I'd better make some fresh coffee for you!" he announced.

Other visits to the old fisherman were made on Mr. Gilmore's rounds. Twice, he was offered checks. Eventually, the old Norwegian decided he might give the local Lutheran church a try again, with Mr. Gilmore's encouragement.

Alex Gilmore used his Irish background—he was born in County Down near Belfast—to help him make friends with other families outside the United Church, including one husband and wife who described themselves as "Roman Catholics hiding from the Pope."

Once, a little girl answered the door. When she saw who it was, she called to her mother: "The man from the church is here. Will I let him in or tell him you're busy?"

As he grew in age, wisdom and experience, Alex Gilmore found himself becoming an unofficial assistant minister.

One Saturday evening, the night before a Christmas service, he got a phone call. His minister at Capilano Highlands was sick. Would he take the main service at 11:15 the next morning?

"The church was packed," Mr. Gilmore recalls. "When I got up and looked at this sea of 500 faces, my knees were surely shaking. But I started thinking about our minister, lying ill and likely worrying about what was happening to his carefully planned service, so I said a short prayer, and then everything went fine."

Others, finding themselves in his place, might not have been so calm. "I found I had mislaid my notes, so all my prayers had to be extempore!"

Since 1964, Alex Gilmore has lived in the little community of Davis Bay, on what is called B.C.'s "Sunshine Coast." Once again elected elder, he also became a Sunday school teacher, for a class of ten- and eleven-year-old boys and girls. "One has to be on his toes to keep up to them," Mr. Gilmore says with considerable understatement. "I explained one day that the Gospels meant 'Good News' about God." Promptly came the question, "What's the bad news about God?"

His minister, the Rev. James Williamson of Gibsons, B.C., described him at a recent ceremony in his honor as "an outstanding and dedicated member of the church. He's a great fellow, and a beautiful Christian. Thank God for elders like Alex—and I use the word *elder* with both meanings."

"I've seen many changes in the church over the years," replies Alex Gilmore. "But in all that time, I've never met a person I disliked. I have met many whose habits or actions I deplored, and I have had differences of opinion with ministers and other elders, but always, I hope, I have had respect for their opinions, without anger or antipathy towards them. I like people, and I like to help people and to make everyone I meet my friend."

Alex Gilmore hopes he can continue to serve his church and his people for a few years yet. The other day a small neighbor, aged four, asked why he was quitting work in his garden so soon. "Because I'm an old man," said Mr. Gilmore.

"You better watch it or they will put you in the garbage can," said the lad.

Alex Gilmore smiles when he tells that story, and concludes: "I hope I'm not yet at the stage to be put in the garbage can."

Rhea Zakich:

A Riot Set Her Faith on Fire

by Martha A. Lane

Her name is Rhea Zakich. She lives in one of those typical middle-class homes—basketball hoop on the garage and bikes in the driveway—in Garden Grove, California. Until about ten years ago, she had always considered herself an average white suburban housewife.

"I had never had it rough," she explains. "I was never particularly concerned with anyone but myself. My world literally never went beyond the house walls."

Then came the 1965 riots in Watts, a black ghetto of Los Angeles. Rhea saw it all on TV with her two young sons.

"Why do people want to shoot one another and burn down houses?" they asked as they watched. "Why don't white people like black people?" Rhea didn't know. So one day she put the boys in the car and drove to downtown Los Angeles to see for herself.

Rhea had not been active in a church before joining one in 1959, but she didn't consciously attempt to put her faith into action until she saw the hopelessness, desperation, and poverty through her own car window. Suddenly she, too, felt pain and fear and suffering. She felt compelled to do something, but what could a white suburbanite do? She had no specialized skills.

Rhea and a handful of friends returned to the inner city to serve. They rented a ghetto apartment. "You can tell me what it's like to live in the slums, but I can't understand until I've shared a filthy toilet at the end of a hall with forty-two other people," she recalls of the experience.

How do you get acquainted in a neighborhood unlike any you've ever lived in? After a number of unsuccessful attempts at making friends, Rhea took her guitar, sat on a curb, and began to sing. Sure enough, she began to meet the children and to hear questions that got to the very roots of her faith: "Hey, Lady, what is God like?"

For two and a half years the little group of persistent housewives shared their talents with people in the ghetto. They started a day-care center, taught literacy and baby-care classes, planned out-of-the-ghetto trips for children, and so on. The women alternated living in their apartment on weekends. Sometimes Rhea's husband, Dan, and sons, Dean and Darin, shared her weekends in the ghetto. Some nights, they remember, were so hot and noisy and oppressive that they wondered if they could take it until morning.

Rhea took slides of her ghetto apartment and the people she knew as neighbors there. She started receiving invitations to speak.

"I began to realize then that no matter how much of my life I gave to the ghetto, it wouldn't mean much unless I could convince suburban people that they have many of the things inner-city people need, education and encouragement, for example."

But people didn't like Rhea's message, even when she dramatized her experiences through music and skits. Friends stopped visiting. Her family did not understand what she was trying to do. Even her church for a time did not support her. In her confusion and loneliness, Rhea found herself reexamining her Christian commitment: "Not between me and my church, but between me and God as I know him through Christ."

A severe throat ailment put an end to Rhea's reports on the ghetto. For three months she was unable to say a word. She found her forced silence "a beautiful time for evaluating my life and planning ahead." But it, too, was lonely. Again friends quit visiting her, this time because it was so laborious to talk with Rhea.

"I got a magic slate," Rhea recalls. "People would ask me a question, and I'd get all excited and start to write an answer—and found that no one wanted to wait around to see what I thought. People also assumed that, since I couldn't talk, I didn't hear either and didn't have any interest in anything."

Rhea's frustration at not being able to communicate verbally for three months gave rise to an idea for a communications game. "At that time there were no games dealing with interpersonal communication. The idea seemed like divine inspiration," she says. "I wrote down every question I wished people would ask me. Then I wrote down all the questions I wanted to ask but couldn't."

The game, in which players discover the joy of sharing feelings and opinions in a nonthreatening atmosphere is called "the Ungame": there are no winners and no losers.

When Rhea was able to speak again, she saw no need for her new game, until she began noticing how artificial and trivial most conversations are. She made dozens of sets of her game by hand, then tried it out on her family, church groups, and anyone else she could corner. It worked! It helped people talk to each other!

Tell It Like It Is, the Ungame, now is being marketed by the thousands. Teachers, probation officers, husbands and wives, suburbanites and inner-city dwellers, young and old alike have found the game helpful.

For several years now Rhea has felt called to work with small groups. "I believe," she says, "that everyone is unique and special, created by God with a purpose, and endowed with special gifts to use in carrying out his or her purpose. The hard part, sometimes, is to discover our gifts. I'm not sure that we can find them alone. Small groups can be a big help here."

Rhea chose to start her small-group work in suburbia. Her goal is "to encourage people to get acquainted with themselves; to help people discover their purposes in life, their gifts for the world, what they have that no one else has."

Much of Rhea's work has been in four- to six-week workshops on communications. She has led Bible studies and sessions on prayer, parent-child relationships, community.

Through the Ungame and her very spirited yet loving leadership abilities, Rhea Zakich is constantly urging people to grow in new ways. Although she has become known as an "interpersonal specialist," she could better be described simply as a Christian who seeks to remain open to Christ and shares with others where her walk with him has led.

Ron Schipper:

More Than a Football Coach

by Barbara Sagraves

The catalog lists him as athletic director and head football coach, but Ron Schipper of Central College in Pella, Michigan, directs more than athletics and coaches more than football.

For hundreds of young people who have had their lives touched by this man in the fourteen years he has been on the campus, he has been a model for them to pattern themselves after.

He is a fierce competitor, a fighter all the way, a good and honest man who plays football the way he plays life—all out and strictly by the rules.

"Whether you want to become a successful person or a successful Christian, in all cases it takes a deep personal commitment to achieve at the maximum level as God intended," Schipper says.

He cites the many outside pressures on young people growing up today in terms of the easy accessibility of drugs, sex, alcohol; and counter-pressures to succeed academically and, often, athletically.

"It's difficult for a young person to be a real Christian today and it takes a whale of a commitment to succeed," he noted. "He or she needs all the help and guidance one can give."

And give he does, not only to his football team, his students and his colleagues, but also to his church. In addition to serving on the consistory, he is in his eighth year of teaching the high school Sunday school class at Pella's Second Reformed Church. He and his wife Joyce are sponsors for the Senior High Youth Fellowship group as well.

Why does he do it? His job is demanding enough with days often beginning as early as 6:00 a.m. and running well past midnight. Why take on more?

"I enjoy young people," Schipper replies. "I think I can relate to them. Because of my long experience in coaching, twenty-four years now, I've learned enough watching them grow up that I think I have something to offer youngsters today. Most of them are looking for a source of direction, and opinions from someone other than their parents and teachers. I can give them that."

Ron Schipper is a native of Zeeland, Michigan, a graduate of Hope College (where he played quarterback on the football team), and the recipient of a master's degree from the University of Michigan. He and his wife, Joyce, have three children.

Prior to coming to Central College in 1961, he coached at the Northville (Michigan) High School and at the Jackson (Michigan) High School. At Northville his teams compiled a 39-5-1 record, with four league championships.

In fourteen seasons at Central, Schipper's record of 101 victories as against 25 defeats and 2 ties, places him at the top of all current collegiate coaches with ten or more years' experience. And in 1974, his Flying Dutchmen captured the NCAA Division III national championship.

"I've had plenty of chances to go other places," he admits, "but I've stayed at Central because of the people. At a school this size I deal with students, not just football players, and we get tremendous support from the entire college and the community of Pella."

Schipper is also dedicated to the concept of intercollegiate athletics. He feels that within athletics, there are great lessons to be learned for life. While he's fully aware of the criticism often directed toward interscholastic competition, he wants to do everything he can to point out the good that can come from such competition.

Reflecting on his recent championship season, Schipper said, "Our seniors gave us tremendous leadership. They had the desire to excel and added a touch of charisma to the whole team. Their commitment was the hidden ingredient in our success, making it a very special season. The chances of that happening again, immediately, are very slim. You take a positive approach but you're never sure. . . ."

David Henion, one of those seniors on the championship squad, now studying for the ministry at Western Theological Seminary, says of his former coach:

"The man has set an example for me and my teammates in word and deed. He has a unique philosophy not only about football but also about being a winner in life. His dedication, self-sacrifice, and self-denial have shown in his professional, family, and spiritual life. I thank the Lord for knowing and working with Coach Schipper and for the opportunity to serve with him on God's squad."

For Schipper, coaching is a very special job. He calls it "the greatest job on earth."

"There have been lots of pleasures and lots of disappointments," he says, "but life is like that. You work hard, you prepare, and sometimes it all blows up in your face. But you have to come back after a defeat. That's exactly what life is, and it's the coming back that make both coaching and living the challenges they are."

A Monday Morning Writer of Letters:

Words Can Make a Difference

by Don Jennings

For more than twenty years I have written at least two Monday morning letters to persons who have inspired me the past week.

This morning one letter went to a well-known television star. His program, as usual, was an inspiration to me. Although he has gained national fame, he had to overcome many problems in his earlier career. His program deserved a word of appreciation.

Not all of my Monday morning letters go to the famous. My second one this morning was a letter of commendation to the choir director of the church where we worship. She and her husband are from Taiwan. He is a college professor; she is well educated in music and has a fine talent in leadership. I told her I appreciate what she is doing with our choir.

Why did I start writing Monday morning letters? It was because I have learned that a word of encouragement, given at the right time, helps each one of us. How true are these words: "It is more blessed to give than to receive."

Wheeler McMillen, a good friend and for many years the editor of a well-known national magazine, once asked me what response came from my Monday morning letters. About seventy-five percent of the recipients, men and women in all walks of life, have responded. But my letters are not written in order to get letters in return.

I do not limit Monday morning letters to adults. I also write to young people. One lad who played an accordion solo one night didn't do well because of inexperience. A personal note praised him for his determination and willingness. I encouraged him to keep it up. His mother told me how her son's face lit up as he read my letter. "To think," he said, "that Mr. Jennings would write and compliment me. I'll show him someday that I can do it." Needless to say, he did that very thing.

In my files is a letter from a well-known radio and television star. He said something one evening that showed he was not ashamed to stand up for the ideals in which he believed. I did not expect the following reply from him:

"We get lots of mail finding fault with things we do and say," he wrote. "We want you to know that it is truly refreshing to get words of commendation. It makes us feel that we want to try harder to live up to the kind words such as you have sent us." The letter was from Arthur Godfrey.

I wrote to a successful, nationally known merchant, telling of the inspiration I had received from his *Lines of a Layman* and from the influence of his life upon so many people.

A few days before his death J. C. Penney responded: "When I think of your practice of writing Monday morning letters, it makes me wonder what would really come to pass if all of us would take up this practice."

It takes only a moment to speak words of appreciation. It takes a little longer to sit down and write a letter. The letter which you take the time to write may mean the difference between defeat and victory to someone.

In a community where I formerly lived, I visited a mother and father whose only son, a soldier, had been killed in action overseas. The mother showed me letters they had received from three of their sons buddies, and I took down their addresses.

I wrote to each of those three men, commending him for his thoughtfulness. One expressed gratitude for my having taken time to write, but he did not let it go at that. A most appropriate card came from him the following Christmas.

One does not need to give an address, sing a solo, be an outstanding official or professional person to be worthy of an appreciative letter. In fact, it often is some little thing that a person does, not expecting praise, that merits a letter of approval.

There have been many Monday morning letters, and it is I who have gained. It is not only the response I have received but the warmth that comes from writing these letters.

The time is short! Tomorrow may be too late. Do it now. Such are the words of advertisements urging readers to take advantage of certain opportunities. How many times we put off writing that letter. We know that we should make that call on a sick friend. That word of praise to a wife or husband is long overdue, even though he or she may know how we feel. Tomorrow may be too late. Yes, do it now!

Jan Gallagher:

Mission on a Motorcycle

by A. Jean Lesher

Jan Gallagher is a petite, graceful woman with a face full of smiling dimples. You wouldn't suspect that she has chalked up 38,000 miles of motorcycle travel. Or that she is the first person to cross one of the Australian deserts alone on a motorcycle. Or that she has ridden the "impassable" bandit-infested trails of southern Colombia.

But she has. And crowded a lot more experiences into her 34 years. She's had her ups and downs, but has remained unwavering in her efforts to help in persons some of the underprivileged of the world. It's not that she doesn't trust charitable institutions (She's a member of St. John's Lutheran Church, Sacramento, California, and has been a member of the Peace Corps), but rather that she sees so many needs that the projects consume all of her energies.

"You'd never think Jan would take on some of these things," says Pastor Jerald R. Ramsdell. "She appears to be timid, but when you get to know her, you're amazed at her strength of character and her willingness to stand up for what she believes."

Jan Gallagher would probably be a pastor today if the Lutherans had been ordaining women when she was graduated from college. Instead, she's an artist with a high sense of human concern. Her current project is to improve the standard of living among impoverished Incan Indians in Guayaquil, Ecuador. Her efforts, which are admittedly meager in the face of the overwhelming poverty, will nonetheless help save lives in an area where eight out of ten children die before age three.

An exhibit of her paintings has been held at the Pacific Lutheran Seminary in Berkeley, and she has met with students and faculty to discuss her concerns. An art shop opened recently in Carmel, California, to which she has imported handmade Incan blankets, ponchos, bags, belts and jewelry to be sold by the newly incorporated, nonprofit Inca-Ecuador Committee headed by Pastor Ramsdell. Several circles in St. John's Church are sponsoring Inca Indian children for $15 a month under the committee's Godparent Plan.

But that's getting ahead of the story. How does the daughter of a naval officer who got used to moving every year discover a poverty pocket in Ecuador and begin these projects? It's a twelve-year odyssey.

Jan left school after five semesters at Midland Lutheran College, Fremont, Nebraska, to travel and work in Europe. During that time, she read about the newly formed Peace Corps. In 1962, she went to Ecuador with the corps to work among the poverty-stricken Indians of Daule. Soon she met a priest, Father Carlos Cuadrado, the son of an Incan princess.

The fifty-five-year-old priest encouraged Miss Gallagher to sponsor the education of a local boy, Bolivar Moran, in the United States when her Peace Corps term ended in 1964. In order to get him there, she traded in her own plane ticket home, bought a Suzuki 250 motorcycle and began the 6,000-mile trek north with 100-pound Bolivar and 200 pounds of supplies, including all of her worldly goods. Jan knew nothing about motorcycles, had no spare parts except spark plugs, and maps were unavailable. But there was only one road, so off they went.

"Bolivar and I figured the roads north couldn't possibly be worse than they were in Ecuador," she recalls. "We were wrong."

It took them two months. During that time they ate one meal a day and generally stayed at night in the homes of friendly villagers. Once they were caught at night on a road in southern Colombia where guerrilla bandits were robbing and killing people. A truck picked them up and brought them safely to a village. Another time the road turned to slippery mud and a truck slid down sideways behind them, gracefully passing them by.

When they arrived in California, Miss Gallagher enrolled Bolivar in school in Sacramento where her parents lived. She then spent two years at the University of California in Berkeley, earning a degree in art while working in the ghettos of East Oakland in a War on Poverty program.

In 1966, Jan went to South Korea with her new husband, a fellow Peace Corps worker, and spent a year and a half as a teacher. The marriage didn't work out, and she returned to Berkeley with a new motorcycle from Japan. With an artist friend from the Lutheran Student Center, Lynne Geries, she took off for Latin America and Europe in October, 1968.

Jan arrived in Ecuador for "a friendly visit" with her friend, Father Carlos. She left the country three months later as an advocate of "peaceful revolution" after seeing that "the poor were only getting poorer" and that Father Carlos and his brothers, sisters and other members of his family seemed to be the only ones who cared. He was heading a project in Guayaquil aimed at providing housing and medical care for uprooted Incan Indians.

But even with the priest's efforts, Jan noted, "Many of the people became thieves in order to live. Children are sent out to steal food or something to sell for food and told not to come home until they get it. They have no water supply, electricity, sewage or garbage service. For a toilet they cut a hole in the floor of their squatter homes which are built on stilts. It's a wretched place!"

Despite this, Miss Gallagher was impressed by the faith of the Cuadrado family. "It was a fantastic experience to see them take the gospel literally and apply it, like, do not be concerned about your own life or what you're going to wear and what you're going to do because God will provide."

Jan left Guayaquil with a promise to replace Father Carlos's pickup truck which had "expired" during her visit. It took her four years to make good on that promise.

Those years brought her and her motorcycle through Europe, Asia and finally to Australia. But she was discouraged by her inability to save enough money from odd jobs or from painting sales to send to Father Carlos. Church organizations greeted her pleas with indifference. "I felt pretty depressed," she said. "I was tired of people asking me why I did what I did and why I didn't settle down."

But after spending one Christmas in Perth, Australia, Jan decided to go across the continent to Sydney, a decision which eventually brought her and her cause to the public eye.

To save money, Jan was determined to drive across 2,000 miles of the Nullarbor Plain. No one had ever done that with a loaded motorcycle.

"I never expected to make it," she recalls.

The motorcycle didn't break down, although it overheated frequently in the 110-degree weather. Her two-week journey attracted a lot of attention. This led to newspaper stories and television appearances where she told the story of Father Carlos and the long-awaited truck.

Much to her surprise, within two weeks she had $2,000 to send to Ecuador. And, unknown to her, a Catholic relief agency in Germany had finally decided to send a Ford pickup to Father Carlos. She also raised enough money to purchase land where Guayaquil slum dwellers could relocate and start farming. A used Land Rover truck was donated for the project, loaded with medical supplies and lapidary equipment for the Incans to make jewelry. And six university-educated Australians decided to pay their way to Ecuador to donate their work for a year.

In the meantime, Jan took a ship home to spend Christmas, 1972, with her parents, Commander and Mrs. Charles Gallagher, in San Diego. "I had promised my parents I'd be home for Christmas," she said, "but I was a couple of years late." Then she went to Ecuador to greet the six Australians.

Since then, Miss Gallagher has continued her fund-raising expeditions in the States. She hopes to cut a commercial record of Incan folk songs and further exhibits of her paintings are planned. After she and Father Carlos visited the University of Arizona in Tucson, the Lutheran campus congregation sent $350 to purchase medicines. "We're still in the process of developing a support group here," says Pastor Lary G. Misner. "But we have four families who support a child on a monthly basis."

Pastor William K. Harman of Our Saviour Lutheran Church in Tucson was chairman of the Youth Convo at the Pacific Southwest Synod meeting recently where Miss Gallagher presented her story. He reports that he had never seen the young people so enthusiastic. They donated $1,200 after hearing Miss Gallagher speak.

"Both my wife and I feel that Jan's chief quality is that she is free—maybe 'liberated' is the word today," says Pastor Harman. "She sees the whole world as her family. She can do her thing anywhere, totally released from the 'things' that tie the rest of us down."

Jan Gallagher, though, points to another source. "If things depended on me, these efforts wouldn't get anywhere. The reason it works is because of Someone else."

Edward L. Rada:

Building a Bridge Across the Pacific

by Andrew Hamilton

One spring evening in 1961, Professor Edward L. Rada of the University of California, Los Angeles, read a newspaper article about Soochow University. Established in 1900 and once known as the "Harvard of Asia," it had become a refugee institution when the Japanese, and later the Communists, took over mainland China. Now, Professor Rada learned, the Methodist-related school was trying to make a physical and academic comeback in Taipei, Taiwan.

"That's it!" Professor Rada announced to his wife, Esther, and their four sons, Steve, Bill, David, and Eddie. "We're going to Taiwan."

Due for a sabbatical leave from UCLA, he wrote that night to Soochow University's president, Dr. C. Y. Stone, a distinguished Chinese scholar who is a law graduate of Michigan and Yale: "This is an opportunity I have long been seeking. I can teach marketing, management economics, and if you wish, even try my hand at English."

President Stone promptly offered the professor a position. Soon the Radas were on their way to Taipei.

Without knowing it, the UCLA economist and member of Holliston United Methodist Church in Pasadena, California, where he is now lay leader, had been preparing for teaching in Taiwan since 1943-46. Then statistical officer for a U.S. Navy maintenance squadron stationed at the Oakland Naval Station, Lieutenant Rada had watched pilots returning from the "mysterious Orient." He had kept records on planes, read pilots' logbooks, listened wonderingly as flyers told tales of adventure in the Pacific and China-India-Burma theaters.

Later, this tug toward the Far East was intensified in his civilian life. After graduate studies at Stanford University, he spent two years as an economist at the University of Hawaii. One of his projects in Hawaii was serving as consultant to Chinese orchid growers.

Until 1937, Soochow University was located in Kiangsu province on the Chinese mainland. It achieved an outstanding reputation in law and biology; many of its graduates became leading jurists and statesmen, physicians and scientists. When the Japanese invaded China in 1937, the campus was moved to Chungking, where it functioned for several years, then to Shanghai after the war. In 1949, the university was closed by the Communists. Alumni reactivated it in 1951 in its present location on Taiwan, and in 1954, it was reaffiliated with the Methodist Church.

Soochow's present 40-acre campus is situated in the beautiful Shih-Lin Valley (The Valley of Culture), a twenty-minute ride from the center of Taipei. Nearby, amid hibiscus and acacia, the government has located the National Palace Art Museum, motion-picture studios, and the soon-to-be-built National Library.

But when the Radas reached Taipei in 1961, the picture was not all that rosy. Soochow University, the professor recalls, was a bleak, "bare-bones place" with concrete floors, paint peeling from the walls, and worn seats and blackboards.

"Even President Stone was using a desk the Salvation Army would have rejected," says Professor Rada.

At that time the campus consisted of seven small buildings: a classroom-administration structure, a student center, a combination auditorium-library-cafeteria building, two dormitories (one for boys, one for girls), President Stone's house, and one other faculty residence.

The 1,000 students then enrolled lived mostly in Taipei and commuted by bus or bicycle. "Except for classroom lectures," says Professor Rada, "there was little contact between students and teachers. Faculty members were so underpaid they had to rush off to other teaching jobs immediately after class. I was one of the few who stuck around."

Coming from UCLA's beautiful campus, Professor Rada saw many things that needed improvement, including faculty pay, inadequate buildings and equipment, and the curriculum. But such improvements cost money.

While in Taipei, Professor Rada presented nine public lectures for which the Chinese Trade and Productivity Center paid him $500. He donated $250 of this to help establish the Chinese Association for the Advancement of Management and $250 to Soochow University itself.

As he accepted the two checks, President Stone called them "the first gifts from the friends of Soochow."

"Friends of Soochow?" asked Professor Rada, somewhat puzzled. "I don't understand. I'm only one person. What can I do?"

"I can't tell you," said President Stone. "It has to be your own commitment. Do as the spirit moves you."

Returning to the United States at the end of his sabbatical, Professor Rada mulled over his experiences and what President Stone had said about the friends of Soochow. He discussed Soochow and its problems with Robert Rogers, then UCLA's assistant vice-chancellor for finance who had made a brief stop in Taipei on a trip to Indonesia. Other Methodist friends and Soochow alumni—former missionaries, teachers, doctors, economists, government officials, business people—were drawn into the circle. One of the most helpful was Don W. Odell, an attorney for the California Teachers Association, who helped prepare incorporation papers for the Friends of Soochow.

This group became a nonprofit, volunteer organization in 1964. In fund-raising and friend-making, the Friends of Soochow, now 650 members strong, have provided opportunities for many Chinese students to obtain an education at Soochow University and abroad; established exchange opportunities for American students and scholars; and built a bridge of cultural and economic understanding between the United States and the Far East.

The first exchange student was Wei-Hsiung ("Kitty") Chow, whom Professor Rada had met at Soochow in 1961-62. With an interest in literature, an excellent command of English, and some teaching experience, she came to the U.S. to earn a master's degree.

Mr. Rogers arranged for a waiver of fees at UCLA, and he and his wife, Mary, found a spare room for her in their home near the campus. She earned extra money by working in the UCLA library and the English department. After receiving her master's degree, she married Dr. Robert Wu, a physicist who now teaches at the U.S. Naval Academy in Annapolis.

A number of private donors and foundations, as well as the Friends of Soochow, have created scholarships and research grants. Professor Rada, a persuasive letter writer and tireless speaker, continues to explain the needs of Soochow and how others can help.

"An individual will contribute $200; a business firm, $1,000; a foundation, $2,500," he says. "It all adds up." He donates $100 a year for the Edward L. Rada Prize, which goes to the best Soochow graduating senior in accounting and economics.

One fund-raising device that is both enjoyable and profitable is the annual meeting of the Friends of Soochow in a restaurant in Los Angeles's Chinatown. After a dinner, eaten with chopsticks, Mr. Rogers auctions off fifteen or twenty art objects that have been donated.

"Here is a wood carving of reclining Liu Hai, Chinese symbol of happiness. More than 100 years old. Minimum price $85. What am I bid?" The price jumps in spirited bidding to $120.

After a little more than a decade in Taiwan, Soochow University has increased its enrollment to 5,000 students and quadrupled the number of campus buildings. More are under construction or in the planning stage. The aim is to rebuild the university's academic "Harvard in Asia" distinction in law and science.

The basic impetus for this effort was considerable financial aid from what now is the United Methodist Board of Global Ministries, some of which Soochow University will repay. United States seed money has also enabled Soochow to build a Graduate School of Economics and Business in downtown Taipei. It houses a computer center.

Three years ago the Friends of Soochow organized a summer session for American students at the university, an idea suggested earlier by President Stone. The term lasts for eight weeks and costs $510 for room, tuition, and a cultural tour of Taiwan. (Transpacific transportation and meals are extra and must be arranged independently.) The summer session includes courses in Chinese art, history, culture, and language.

"It is as important for Americans to travel to the Far East, as I discovered myself, as it is for Chinese students to come to the United States," Professor Rada says. "The Pacific basin is one of the significant areas of the world, and it is essential for young people to understand it." Professor Rada is an authority on health and consumer economics, world population and food, and the economics of health and medical care. He is now with UCLA's School of Public Health.

Most summer term students are from the West Coast and Hawaii, but they're not all of the younger generation. One was sixty-nine-year-old Karleen Hoffman of San Diego, who attended the 1972 session. "Working and living with young people was a lot more fun than being stuck in a rest home," she said.

Shelby and Dorothy Simmons, a Los Angeles couple in their mid-fifties, attended the 1972 summer session. Shelby was an engineer at an aircraft corporation, and Dorothy was a home-economics teacher in the Van Nuys public schools. They had been thinking of joining the Peace Corps but have gone back to Soochow University to teach and to help.

Like most support groups, the Friends of Soochow in its formative period set up various designations according to membership support. The top category ($10,000 or more) was easy: They're Eternal Friends. But what to call those in the lowest category ($5 to $10)? "They're Good Friends," says Professor Rada.

The Friends of Soochow include many friends by whatever designation. And one of the best is Professor Edward L. Rada.

Single Parent:

Finding a Place in the Big City

by Pauline Miller

"Come Saturday Morning"—this was the song Damian and I used to sing when he was two months old, and it seems as if our life from then on was in the spirit of the song, he and I journeying through life together. Bringing up a child single-handed in New York City can be a grueling experience, especially when the child is of the opposite sex. But through all our difficulties and sorrows Damian and I have maintained a feeling of great joy in each other and have shared happiness in our adventures. It is this joy that predominates, in spite of the demands and the pitfalls.

Because there is no spouse with whom I share affection, the bond between us, mother and son, is close and intimate. Damian, now four-and-a-half years old, and I share our problems, our feelings, our expectations and our sadnesses with complete freedom.

Damian is a sensitive child. Though as active and boisterous as any child of his age, he is unusually articulate and in touch with his feelings. Of course, as with any pleasure, the relationship has to be watched and I am aware of the danger of it becoming too close.

Certain difficulties come up. For instance, I find myself preferring to stay at home and take care of house and child rather than seek new possible life partners. And, of course, financial problems—baby-sitting fees being expensive—present an immediate excuse. However, as Damian gets older and more independent my life seems to be opening out. An easier solution for me has been to keep him constantly in the company of other children and to give him as large a supply of adults as possible to see as models and with whom to learn to form good relations.

With this in mind, my first step, when my husband left us to go to California to look for acting work, was to take Damian home to my parents in England. Here, in a small country village he was able to live with another father-and-mother figure for a while and make friends with other children in the neighborhood. Once we were back in New York after six months, such support was far more difficult for us to find. But I was fortunate in getting a place for him in a day-care center and nursery school called Prescott House. Here we enjoyed many advantages available to a single parent alone with a child in a large city. Damian immediately had children of his own age to play with all day. He had trained teachers who were sensitive and devoted to these sometimes insecure children. At Prescott House there was a strong principle of love and fellowship, at odds with big-city indifference, at the heart of the school's every activity.

Every three weeks, parents and teachers would get together in group therapy sessions under the leadership of Ava Sigler, an analyst, to talk over their various problems and insecurities. Ava's help was invaluable and there was comfort in discovering that one's three- or four-year-old's antics were quite normal after all.

My own son, for instance, will talk nonstop in ever more piercing tones and generally become an out-and-out pest until I pull myself together and admit to him that I am feeling sad (he understands this emotion better than "worried") at which point he will always asks why. And with that we find ourselves talking on a deep level which in itself will often disperse the circles of worried chatter within my mind.

Of course there are still times when the situation grows to unbearable proportions. Then I know that I have to have some time alone, and I endeavor to find another parent willing to "swap" children. She—or occasionally he, as there are single fathers as well as single mothers—will pick Damian up from school, take him home where he will eat, play and sleep, and then transport him to school again in the morning. In return I will do the same. I am aware, when I am plainly not coping with the situation, that it is essential to separate myself from Damian in order that he won't feel the full force of my insecurity and will be able to draw on another adult's strength for a while. Once I am sure he is occupied and happy, I can devote all my energy to finding my own equilibrium. As a result we return to one another refreshed.

Of course, the other valuable advantage of the sessions with Ava Sigler is the chance to get together in a group and not feel the tremendous isolation which is often the plight of the single parent. Our membership in the Fifth Avenue Presbyterian Church has helped us enormously in this respect. It has a warm congregation and here we are welcomed as into a family. Damian looks forward to the Sunday School all week and I to the support of an enlightened ministry, whose help I sought more than once in time of need, and a coffee hour preceding the service at which people can meet each other and chat for a while. Discovering its value has led several of my single parent friends to join its membership, though as yet we have had little time to give to the many projects in which it is involved. Earning a living, running a home, and bringing up a child does not leave one with much time to spare! I can see now how sensible it is to have a partner with whom one can share the chores and the responsibilities!

At the end of a year's stay at Prescott, Damian was lucky enough to be selected as the one child in his year to be admitted to the entry tests for the Hunter Elementary Program. Later I found out he had been chosen to attend this school.

This was wonderful news as it meant he was guaranteed an exceptional education at no financial burden to me. He is now in his fifth month at Hunter, where he learns arithmetic, how to read and write, and does innumerable projects from 8:30 a.m. till 12:45 p.m., has lunch, an hour and a half nap, and plays in a day-care program until I pick him up, usually around 4 p.m. Once again he has a solid, imaginative, and highly creative atmosphere in which to spend his days, which helps to make up for the lack of a family at home and to give him the security and attention he needs.

I take Damian to and from school, and in fact almost everywhere we go together, on the back of my bicycle. It is a fast, convenient and economical way for the two of us to get around. We will often come straight home from school. I like to prepare nourishing meals made from organic vegetables and health foods and never cut corners when it comes to feeding Damian. Then we have time to spend together. There are many activities we enjoy: painting, making Christmas and birthday cards, or simply coloring or painting pictures; we listen to records; we both enjoy singing and Damian has a particularly accurate ear. We play games like Snakes and Ladders, Dominoes, or cards. His passion at the moment is wrestling, and I am receiving daily instruction in Kung Fu! Perhaps his favorite occupation, however, is helping me with some job which needs doing around the apartment—anything from unscrewing screws while we mend a lamp, to sweeping the dust into a dustpan, to washing the dishes.

Before he goes to sleep, I read one of his many books to him. This is a magic moment of the day, for we share a love of fantasy and words. I taught him the alphabet at an early age and now as I read, I help him to understand how words are constructed, their root meanings, and their various uses. I introduce him to the dictionary, to the maps of the world and to an awareness of different languages and different ways of living.

I like him to understand that people have different habits and different ways of expressing themselves. This is one of the benefits of growing up in New York. Here he rubs shoulders with every color and creed and is richer for the experience. Before he goes to sleep, I sing to him. Often, then, he will talk to me about something that is on his mind—perhaps the mystery of what God is thinking, or the absence of his father and of how sad this makes him. One night recently he said, "You know, Mummy, I always sleep with my eyes open." "Oh, why's that?" I asked him. "Well, my Daddy might come home and if I shut my eyes I might miss him."

Of course, it's difficult to deal with one's own emotion at a time like this. I generally try to reassure him by telling him again that his father is away from him as he had to find work, that he loves him very much and that they will see each other again soon. I then attempt to direct his thoughts to an activity the following day which I know he will enjoy. I realize, too, that there is a sadness which cannot be denied, and sometimes I say that everybody is sad sometimes and that it is all right to be sad.

Damian is concerned about the fact that I am alone and will question me about whether I am married or not and whether I am going to be married. The other day he cornered a neighbor of ours and suggested that he come and live with us as he, Damian, needed a father and his own Daddy was taking too long to come back from California!

I make no secret of the fact that our situation is not quite as it should be. But like Pollyana, I always remind Damian of something we can feel happy about and remind him, too, of his friends who are having similar if not more difficult problems than ours. He understands quite well that Dee, a friend of his from Prescott, has neither a father nor a mother but now has a Daddy who has adopted him.

Last summer, in order to bring more people into our relationship, I spent some time at a spiritual school and community in Long Island. Here Damian ran free with the children of the community over their extensive grounds, climbing trees, making dens, and surprising rabbits, chipmunks and other small creatures, while I worked alongside the other community members. We ate, slept, and lived there, and I discovered a new way to self-discipline and strength through the practice of Yoga, which I learned in the school.

The lack of the support of a community in a big city is the most distressing thing about being a single mother. Society tends to be indifferent, at best, except in the rare and wonderful instances I have mentioned, and the problem of finding friends for myself and Damian has been difficult. Searching for other children for Damian to play with, I am often in the company of a married couple. This frequently becomes uncomfortable, as the wife finds herself threatened by an unattached female. On the other hand, single males are likely to be out of touch with children, impatient with their behavior, and resentful of the time and attention they require. Of course, other single parents have the same kind of problems and here we are accepted—but the magnitude of pressures has usually resulted in neurosis in child and parent, and an atmosphere of anxiety.

There were times when I was completely at a loss to know what to do for the best, and I count myself as one of the more fortunate who found help. My concern is for other young mothers I met along the way. There are few places like Prescott House and Hunter to aid in rearing a child and while I was searching for day-care facilities I came across some grim situations.

In one case, two young people, out of work, were baby-sitting five or six young children in a small windowless apartment with few or no amenities. The two- and three-year-olds were already troubled by the loss of one parent. They were often sick, with heavy colds, stomach upsets, and other things, and the young people caring for them had no experience of child-rearing and little knowledge of these tiny beings' requirements. The atmosphere was one of fear and tension. I am sure the mothers who left their children here had little other choice.

Another vivid memory is of a harassed social worker in a city day-care center sending a three-year-old home for lack of toilet training. Of course the mother was working, trying to act as a provider, and had not had time to train the child properly. She would now have to leave her work to pick up the child, losing at best a day's pay and at worst her job, and the whole process of finding care for her child and work for herself would begin over again.

Damian, however, is now no longer a baby. We have passed those hurdles, and for better or worse he is equipped for a continuing challenge. I attempt to pass on to him a feeling of stability, faith, and courage. It was hard to face with him the gaping hole where there should have been husband, father, and family, but it was almost as if we made the decision to accept life's limitations together and to learn that when the scene is not set exactly as one would have liked, the question is "What to do now?" and the answer as we found it, is to make the best of what there is, enjoy it and keep learning!

Lillian Willoughby:

Turning the Other Cheek Means Caring

by Richard K. Taylor

When I saw my friend struck hard across the face, I thought immediately of Jesus' words about turning the other cheek. Have you ever wondered whether it really makes sense to follow that pointed command, "If any one strikes you on the right cheek, turn to him the other also?"

Lillian Willoughby is in her mid-fifties, with strong Quaker convictions. She has spent a lifetime raising a family, working as a nutritionist, and supporting projects on peace and social justice. We live about three blocks from each other in an area of old row houses in West Philadelphia.

A few weeks ago, I was awakened at 4:00 a.m. by a phone call from a friend whose worried voice told me that something was very wrong. His thirty-year-old sister, whom I'll call Anne, has been having bouts of mental illness for the past two years. "She's very upset," he said. "I think she may need to go back to the mental hospital. She got up about an hour ago. She's been wandering around the house, talking loudly, and she's been spilling water from the sink onto the floor. Do you think you could get someone and come out to help?"

Lillian had known Anne for many years, so I didn't hesitate to call her. I woke her from a sound sleep, but she quickly agreed to go with me. Within a few minutes we were on our way to Anne's suburban house. It was comforting to have Lillian sitting beside me, her short figure wrapped in a warm woollen shirt and her greying hair held back by a ribbon. I was glad to be able to talk with her about what we might do to help.

At the house we expressed our friendship and support to Anne, and this seemed to calm her. I was reassured to see some steadiness come back into her pretty face, although the occasional far-away look in her dark eyes warned me that something was still wrong.

Later in the morning we went with Anne to see her psychiatrist. He talked with her and then told us that it should be possible to keep her at home on a careful schedule of medication. "We'll use the hospital only if she starts losing control again," he said. "If she does need hospitalization, I hope she'll agree to enter voluntarily. That would show that she recognized her need for treatment."

The plan of staying at home seemed feasible. Anne's brother, a bright, sensitive young man who had just graduated from college, said that he could stay with her for at least a few months.

Lillian and I went home feeling encouraged. After the visit, Anne seemed much more composed and rational.

But when I decided to check by phone later in the afternoon, I found that she had suffered a complete breakdown. Even over the phone I could hear her violently stamping her feet in another room. "Please get Lillian and come out as fast as you can," her brother urged.

I called Lillian, who turned the supper-making over to her husband, and we drove as fast as we could to Anne's house. We knew that Anne's turbulent, uncontrolled mood might make it hard to reach her. We both felt the need for God's strength, so when we parked the car, we paused for a moment of silent prayer. My eyes were still shut when I heard Lillian say, "Here they come." I looked up and saw Anne and her brother coming through the field across from the house.

They came over a little rise. It seemed at first that they were just walking slowly and holding hands. But then I saw Anne lean back and yank hard at her brother's hand, as if she were trying to get away. We found later that Anne had rushed out of the house and had been screaming and running back and forth through the field. Her brother was afraid that she might dart out into the busy highway, and he was trying to restrain her and get her back indoors.

We walked up to them and Lillian took Anne's free hand and said, "We're here now, don't worry, it's all right." But Anne was much too distraught to listen. She snatched her hand away and stood shaking, glaring furiously at Lillian.

Suddenly she hit Lil hard—crack!—across the face. A few stunned seconds passed. The slap seemed to reverberate in the air. The spot on her cheek must have stung; I expected Lil at least to rub it, if not to grab Anne and try to avoid another smack. But she stood still and said in a gentle but firm voice, "Would you like to hit the other one?"

Anne's eyes looked very bright. Her mouth twisted into a fierce half-smile. It almost seemed as if Lillian's words challenged her. Her open hand came up. She hit Lillian hard on the other cheek, paused for a second, and then swung back her arm full length and hit her with another terrific slap.

Somehow Lil kept her arms at her sides. But it must have been really painful, and in a moment she hung her head and began to cry. She sobbed softly. The tears ran down her cheeks. Anne looked closely at Lil. The wild intensity in her face faded slowly into a look of puzzlement. She seemed to be grappling with something inexplicable. Suddenly, a look of real concern came into her eyes. I think for the first time she really saw her friend, Lillian, and realized that she was hurting. She stepped forward and put her arms around Lil, and they held each other for a minute, with Lil saying through the tears, "It's O.K., it's all right."

Soon we were able to walk Anne back across the highway to the house. We sat down in the kitchen and talked and ate and kept giving warm support to Anne until she was again able to calm herself. Later that evening, we checked again with the doctor, and then drove her to the hospital where she had stayed before. As he had hoped, she voluntarily signed herself in.

When I visited Anne a few days later, she was composed and able to take a real interest in our conversation. I think she will be coming home soon.

This experience has made me reflect more deeply on Jesus' words about cheek-turning. I suppose we have all heard people scoff at their supposed "impracticality." "If you turn one cheek," they say, "you'll just get busted on the other one, and what good will that do?"

And it's true—Lillian did get hit again, not once, but twice.

But Lillian didn't allow those hard slaps to be the whole story. When she turned her other cheek, and cried with the pain, but kept reaching out to Anne, she expressed a caring which communicated itself. It broke into Anne's uncontrolled behavior and enabled her finally to express her own caring in response.

Cheek-turning, it seems, is not an action to be followed by rote. It is rather, at times, a necessary part of communicating love to another person.

Did I see in the field near Anne's house, I have asked myself, something of the defenseless, vulnerable, but persistent love which enabled Jesus in his time to face the mentally ill and to heal them? If a person struck me, would I be capable of the outreaching love which Jesus, and Lillian, expressed?

Christopher Ballard:

A Child's Gift of Joy

by Marie Coventry

On a beautiful spring day in 1957, a loaded moving van backed up to the door of the empty house directly across the street. The new tenants arrived in a blue station wagon: father, mother, seven-year-old Christopher and Penny, a tiny Mexican Chihuahua. Christopher was in a wheelchair. He could not walk, could not use his hands and arms the way other seven-year-olds could use theirs; couldn't really hold his head very well. But he could smile, he could wave, he could talk. Even before we were properly introduced he was smiling and waving to me from his wheelchair.

It was fortunate for me that he made the first advances as I was in a dreary state of mind, going through what I now think of as the emptipause. Our family was grown and gone and the stimulation of feeling useful seemed to have gone as well. Solitude had taken the form of loneliness, my hobbies had little interest for me, church and community work filled me with excuses, coffee parties bored me.

Then came Christopher with his wheelchair, his wonderful smile, his deep-throated chuckle, his delightful sense of humor, his interest and involvement in almost everything and everyone, his great serenity, and his gift. Certainly at my age I did not expect to receive pointers from a seven-year-old on how to make life more meaningful, especially a seven-year-old in a wheelchair. But that is what happened. For two years I was the pupil and he the teacher, although at the time I didn't realize it. In fact, I supposed our positions to be just the reverse.

He delighted in sharing with me his records, his stamp collection, his own make of cut-out cookies. Although I was old enough to be his grandmother, he loved to inveigle me into a game of pretend hide-and-seek. The more fantastic the places in which we would pretend-hide, the more fun it was. When he would "catch" me at the top of a telephone pole or on the spire of the church he would coax, "Come down slowly, I do like to watch you." And as a courteous afterthought, "and I don't want you to fall." He always gave himself time to enjoy each experience.

I remember one day he was holding a stalk of bluegrass. I had seen thousands of plain old bluegrass but as Christopher twirled that stalk between his thumb and finger, with the sunlight dancing on the seed head bringing out colors of purple, pink, blue and green to make of it a thing of beauty, I realized I had never before actually *seen* bluegrass.

Christopher had his bad days and his good ones. As I look back I realize how carefully he folded up the bad days and spread out the good ones, almost as one would close up or open a parasol. He couldn't go to school but had his daily lessons at the dining-room table, his wonderful mother the self-appointed teacher. Here was an area in which I could be of service and with a certain amount of self-righteousness, I fear (I soon found I was getting more than I was giving), I took my turn with the teaching. He was well ahead of his age group in school and could and did talk of current events, especially sports, with knowledge and zest.

Two years passed by. Christopher was nine, a great favorite in the neighborhood. It was amazing to see the wheelchair boy the center of a group of youngsters, to hear his laugh ring out above all of the others, to have him suggesting new ideas, new interests. In Little League baseball season, we wheeled him to the ball park. He was like a mascot for all the teams and won a place of affection and admiration on that playing field. When the Little Leaguers voted him their most loyal supporter, made him an honorary member of the League and presented him with an autographed baseball he was almost overwhelmed, but not quite! On the way home he remarked, as he held the ball lovingly in his hands, "I'm lucky I have time to be happy; some of the other kids don't."

As I thought of the "other kids" who could run and play ball but perhaps, according to Christopher, hadn't time to know they were happy, I realized how like them I was.

"You've given me a gift, Christopher," I said, "an awareness of joy."

"Who? ME?" asked Christopher.

Soon it was holiday time. Christopher had a great longing to go to Yellowstone National Park, so on a bright morning in August the station wagon was loaded with air mattresses, wheelchair, camping equipment, father, mother, boy, and dog. As I waved them goodbye amid shouts of "Good luck," "See you in two weeks," "Have fun," I was already looking forward to their homecoming, to hearing about their trip as seen through Christopher's youthful, penetrating eyes.

But we didn't see them in two weeks.

Minutes before midnight on Monday, August 17, 1959, an earthquake shook the mountains in and around Yellowstone National Park. We heard the report on the early news Tuesday morning. A lake in southwest Montana had tilted, water had leaped a dam in raging fury; downstream in the Madison River's narrow canyon, a mountain had split. Millions of tons of rock and rubble had fallen on campers at the Rock Creek campgrounds. Many persons were missing.

Because Christopher and his parents had become dear to us, we had been travelling with them, in imagination, for the ten days. We felt a great relief that according to plan the station wagon should be well away from the Rock Creek campgrounds and the Madison slide area.

Then the newspapers came, and we read about a boy in a wheelchair and his parents who were missing, about a boy who had been an inspiration to the other campers, about a boy and his parents who had been camping at Rock Creek on Monday night and could not be found on Tuesday. Some of the survivors told reporters how the campers at Rock Creek had congregated that Monday night around the station wagon from Canada, of the talk and laughter, of the genuine friendliness, of women exchanging addresses and men sharing their fly fishing tactics—and always the boy in the wheelchair—until darkness sent them to their chosen camping places.

Though the names of the victims had not as yet been released, we had little doubt that this was the family that we knew and loved from across our street.

Saturday was a long day, the day they were to return, as I watched for the station wagon that didn't come home. The following week newspapers reported as missing Mr. and Mrs. Ballard and son Christopher of Nelson, British Columbia. (I thought of Penny, too.)

At the memorial service held in the neighboring Anglican Church, Canon Silverwood spoke of the courage, devotion, and zest for life of these three fine people and of the inspiration it had been to him to know them. He spoke what was in my heart.

A blade of grass, a fleecy cloud, a friend, a cut-out cookie, everything in God's world had taken on new meaning as seen through Christopher's eyes, and for two years he had let me look through those eyes. He had given me an everyday awareness of joy. (Who? ME? Yes, YOU, Christopher.)

Eddie Aguilar:

Another Kind of Revolution

by J. Richard Peck

The young revolutionist was surrounded by persons he had once terrorized.

Only five years ago, Eddie Aguilar had helped seize the First Spanish United Methodist Church building in Harlem. Now he stood in the same church. His beard and beret were gone, but people attending the Sunday-morning service would soon know who he was. He was one of the Young Lords who had disrupted their worship services, occupied their building on two occasions, and caused $17,000 in damages. The pastor was not the same man whose sermons had been shouted down, but some of the worshipers now present had been held hostage by the Lords while the church doors were nailed shut with railroad spikes.

It was too late to run. The Rev. Pedro Pablo Piron was introducing Eddie and inviting him to come to the pulpit. Fearfully, Eddie approached the chancel.

"Feel free, you are at home," said Pastor Piron. The encouraging words and a hurried silent prayer gave Eddie the courage he needed, and he stepped into the pulpit.

He began his story hesitantly, telling of his arrival in New York City from Puerto Rico at age ten, the divorce of his parents, his rejection of the church, and his fight for survival in the Puerto Rican ghetto. He told about his life as a member of the Ghetto Brothers, the Persian Knights, and The Strangers, a life that had revolved around sex, drugs, and gang wars. Vietnam veterans instructed the boys in combat techniques. Stealing and getting high on drugs seemed to come naturally.

Shortly after Christmas in 1969, Eddie was told the Young Lords had taken over a church in the El Barrio section of Harlem. "Hey, right on," he said. "Let's go down there."

After undergoing the elaborate security measures that had been set up by the militant Puerto Ricans, Eddie was granted admittance into the barricaded building. There he joined other young men who were discussing Mao Tse-tung and revolutionary theory. Their methodology was to "hit the sacred institutions of America below the belt." Their goal was to achieve independence for Puerto Rico.

Meanwhile, the United Methodist bishop, district superintendents, and pastors were meeting with Young Lords supporters and police to devise a productive and nonviolent response to the occupation. Public debates balanced the right of a congregation to determine its own patterns of worship and service against the church's responsibility to minister to the needs of the community. Eleven long days passed before the occupation was ended with the eviction and arrest of 105 persons.

The matter appeared to be settled until Julio Roldan, a member of the Young Lords, was found hanged in a city jail in October, 1970. Carrying Julio's body and armed with guns, the Lords seized First Spanish Church for a second time. Accusing the city of murder, the Lords demanded that the church building be used as a legal-services center.

By the time the second occupation took place, Eddie had moved to a position of leadership in the Young Lords. Named as an information officer, it was his responsibility to interpret the Lords' revolutionary tactics to city residents. Nearly two months of conversations and bitter controversy passed before a settlement was reached, and the occupation ended in early December, 1970.

Now, five years later, Eddie was standing in the pulpit of the church he once had called an "imposition on the community." Whatever might have been true in the past, the church's Sunday bulletin now carried notices of a day-care center, after-school programs, boxing, wrestling, and baseball activities designed to serve the neighborhood. Eddie found it difficult to believe he once considered these gentle people "Fascists" and "slaves to religion."

He continued his story, telling how, after the second occupation of the church, the Lords had taken over Lincoln Hospital and a televison truck. Those efforts were followed by a gang fight in which many persons were seriously injured. "Things got so hot," said Eddie, "I had to go to Puerto Rico for a few months until everything cooled down."

In Puerto Rico, a cousin begged him to attend church with him. At first Eddie refused all invitations, but the insistent cousin finally got him to attend a discussion and prayer meeting in a neighboring home. A woman led the discussion, which centered on the conversion experience. "I was like Saul," said Eddie. "Money, drugs, and the revolution were my gods. I asked the group to pray for me. As they did so, I felt a peace settle over me. I gave myself to Jesus."

Eddie returned to the United States a changed man. He was still a revolutionist, but he traded his knife and gun for a Bible and a notebook. Drawing upon his knowledge of street life and his experiences as a drug addict, he began his campaign to transform lives. "Hey, bro," he would tell a heroin addict, "snow white's made a slave out of you, and now you are dead. I know someone who can give you life." Outcasts wandering the streets at 3 a.m. found him a sympathetic listener and wise counselor.

Former friends were not so understanding of the changes in their colleague. "That brother used to be so together," they would say. "Now the white man has brainwashed him."

But the Christ Eddie spoke of was not a blue-eyed blond. He was the redeemer of persons of all nationalities. "I had tried to be a hippie, a yippie, a gang member, a Muslim, a Jehovah's Witness," Eddie said. "Through all this there was only emptiness. When I found Christ, I found life."

Members of his former gang were less enthusiastic when Eddie told them he was through with street fights. Others who had left the gang had suffered broken arms and legs. Just what really happened after Eddie told the Ghetto Brothers he was through as their leader is still a mystery. Observers agree that an angry group carrying machetes trapped him in an alley. Eddie claims he simply prayed and walked away. Others report that he suddenly disappeared.

Eddie not only suffered the wrath of his former friends and gang members; his earlier acts against members of opposing gangs were not forgotten either. Julio Rivera, a seventeen-year-old member of the Reapers, remembered Eddie as the man who had seriously injured some of his "brothers." When he learned Eddie was back in the neighborhood, he took a contract to kill him. Julio followed Eddie about, hoping to find a time when he was alone. He discovered Eddie had a job with the New York City Human Resources Center and that he spent a lot of time in churches and on the street talking about his faith. This was not the same young man who had led the vicious Ghetto Brothers.

Julio, who had spent most of his life "robbing and running," could not understand what had happened to Eddie. Finally Julio spoke with him and, surprising himself, agreed to go to a church service with him. After a time, the Julio who had wanted to kill Eddie became a new person in Christ, working in the streets with his former adversary.

Julio was joined by ten other young persons. "Now," reported Eddie to the congregation, "we are still revolutionists. We use guerrilla warfare tactics and systematically invade various communities with the revolutionary news about Jesus Christ."

During the hymn that followed, some of the worshipers wept openly. Then Eddie stepped from the pulpit into the warm embraces of church members.

His future remains uncertain. Perhaps it will be possible for him to continue full time in his street ministry. In any case, Eddie sees the church as a "sleeping giant that could turn the city and the nation around." He believes the revolution has barely begun.

Lydia Dowler:

God Makes a Task Possible

by Nancy Millar

I first met Lydia Dowler as a result of a neighbor's tip. "She'll make a good interview," the neighbor said. "She's just back from the craziest holiday."

I was a bit dubious. How crazy a holiday could a seventy-one-year-old woman have with her seventy-three-year-old husband, and in the middle of winter?

So, with that sort of jaded attitude, I met Lydia Dowler.

She's something else, that lady is. Not that she would know what I was talking about, for she doesn't use modern jargon. She talks about "giving witness" and "glorifying God" and "having the faith of a mustard seed" and other old-fashioned things like that, but of all the modern "with it" people that I've met, she more than anyone "has it all together."

She listens to God. That's the trick, she says—listening. God talks to us all the time, she says, he abides with us (see, that's how she talks) but we don't tune in. We don't pay attention to his divine intentions.

"When I can't sleep, I run over the world and catch people's thoughts," she told me. And one morning recently, she thought of an old music teacher that she hadn't seen nor heard from for years. "Well, God," Lydia said to herself, "you must have put that thought into my mind for some reason." So she got out of bed at 5 a.m. and phoned the woman she had just thought of. "Lydia, how did you know I needed someone?" the old woman asked on long distance. It turned out that indeed she had needed someone to care about her right then.

Incidentally, it was 8 a.m. where the old woman lived. God somehow manages time zones in his connections with Lydia Dowler. And I'm not being flippant. Lydia just knew the old woman needed her, no matter when. Nothing is impossible with God.

She doesn't look holy, if you know what I mean. She wears frilly-dilly clothes and feminine shoes and lets her hair curl becomingly around her face. She doesn't look at all like the women that came out of the Sunday school vans to tell us little frontier youngsters that we ought not to have any heathen images before us. She looks as heathen as the rest of us.

Only she isn't. She lives with God.

It takes some getting used to—at first the whole attitude of "God knows best; He will provide; God is love" is a bit too too nice. I mean, there are babies out there dying for lack of food and love. What are we talking so nicey-nicey for?

But she's not phony. She's just like that. There is no division in her religous self and her own self. She is a believer always.

Why are those babies dying, I ask? How can you believe in a good God when babies die?

God didn't make those babies die, she says. There are droughts and hurricanes and all sorts of natural happenings. Those operate by a law of nature and we aren't able to understand them. But, she said, think of all the hurricanes and famines that didn't come. Think of all the babies that lived. And if we try to do the best we can in this world, maybe fewer babies will have to die.

But, I persist, you can't know there's a God. You can't see him or know for sure.

Pretend that you are blind, she said to me. If I brought you into this living room and said to you, "Sit, there is a chair there," would you sit?

Yes, I said.

Why?

Because you wouldn't hurt me if you could help it.

So it is with God, she said. You can't see but you know and trust.

She and her husband left on their driving holiday to the Panama Canal with that kind of faith. Both had been ill. The doctors shook their heads over these two innocents taking off in the middle of winter to drive a camper all the way from Calgary, Alberta, to the Panama Canal. If cold weather wouldn't get them en route, then the hot climates would on arrival, they predicted.

Nothing got that old pair. Whenever they needed help, they got it. They got lost driving through Mexico City—naturally, who doesn't? Out of the blue came a man who offered to drive them through, for nothing.

The same thing happened in San Salvadore and Managua. People saw their difficulty and met it without asking for reward or thanks. Lydia attributes their "luck" to God—no question about it. They wanted to fly to Peru from Panama but didn't know what to do with the camper. A priest offered space in the grounds of a church. And so on it went; they survived the trip and enriched all those that they met as well as themselves.

"Something stretches in you," Lydia said, remembering the trip, "when you experience things like the Copper Canyon in Mexico. Something stretches and deepens and makes all the worry and uncertainty come right.

"We watched a man and his mule inch along a trail on the side of the Copper Canyon. It just didn't seem possible that he could find room to proceed. It looked as if he's be dashed to the rocks below anytime. But he wasn't. Why then should we worry about getting lost in the middle of a big city?

"I'm not afraid to die anymore; I used to be, but I've worked that out. I don't like the idea that a long hard dying period might bring distress to those who love me. My mother's death took a long time and was very hard on all of us. She begged to be released, but one day after she had been in a coma for weeks, she suddenly became lucid and dictated a letter to my brother. That letter sustained him for the rest of his life. There was a reason for her lingering until that moment. God knows best."

Are we nothing after we die, I ask?

"We are never nothing," she said, with fine disregard for her years of teaching grammar. "Our soul lives on; I don't know how. That's beyond our comprehension."

What's a soul?

"Soul for me is the God in me, soul is the God in people. You can't teach little children all your life without realizing another depth within them, one that can't be described but it's there, especially in very young children who haven't learned to cover up."

Lydia never had any children of her own, but throughout the years she has taught and nurtured many little ones. Her dentist husband served for some years in northern Canada and eventually Lydia found herself teaching Eskimo children. "School was sometimes frightening for these little children," Lydia remembered, "so their wise mothers used to teach them a string game, sort of a cat's cradle game for one. Each child would be taught a slightly different pattern, one that was his or her own. Whenever the child felt lonely or frightened, he would play with his piece of string, reworking again and again his own pattern. By spring, the string could stand up by itself," Lydia smiled at the memory, aware of the loving and giving that went into that simple string game.

"We have to give more in this world," she said. "Not just money, but we need to give feelings, and openness with one another, and help, and love. We should give until it hurts, as they say in the ads."

Does God want us to hurt, I asked? You can see how I looked for the holes in her faith.

"God doesn't want us to be selfish. He will make our tasks possible."

She sounds so much like those easy answers that fill religious pamphlets, but she's genuine. I kept looking at her to see if I could find the cracks, hear doubts. I wanted to rub her to see if she erased.

But she didn't. Lydia is honest to God.

A Congregation:

No Excuses, Just Action

by Janette Pierce

In the winter of 1973–1974 a member of St. Paul's Mission, Bear Mount, near Amherst, Virginia, learned she was to be evicted from her tiny farmhouse. When she and John Haraughty, the Episcopal Church Army lay officer in charge of the mission, got together on the problem, they found that affordable rental housing just didn't exist in the area and that several other families in the congregation faced eviction, too.

Now, not quite two years later, with faith, hope, hard work, and a little help from their friends, these St. Paul's families live in a new community of trim, attractive homes. They not only own their own homes, but—through a community association—they own and manage a 100-acre farm and orchard with the only operating cider press in that apple growing area of southwestern Virginia.

Something is right about those folk owning an apple orchard on Long Hill Mountain. According to Capt. Haraughty's research, most of the congregation is Indian, probably Monacan, a tribe that stayed in Virginia when the rest of the eastern Sioux went west. And for several generations Indian families have worked local orchards which belonged to others.

Life hasn't been easy for most native Americans in the East or in the West, and the community here is a close-knit one. Family ties are obvious in the predominance of Branhams and Johns among the surnames in the mission's records.

To start looking for one rental property and end with a housing development and an operating farm and orchard could seem unusual, but not if you know John Haraughty and St. Paul's. It's definitely a mission on the move.

When a place to rent appeared impossible to find, John Haraughty went with Lucian and Gene Branham, a father-and-son team from his congregation, to call on local landowners. The Branham men had a special stake because the apple archard where they lived and worked was about to be sold.

The search was discouraging: land was for sale but at speculator prices and in larger parcels than the 30 acres the congregation needed and hoped it could afford. The group's last hope was to call on the Branhams' landlord. An active Baptist layman, William Burrus was sympathetic. He had already agreed to sell his orchard to a returning veteran but urged the Branhams to look at other land he owned.

After search and discussion, the congregation decided on some alternatives, and the three men returned to Mr. Burrus. He told them the previous sale had fallen through. "I just have the feeling I should give you that orchard. It just seems like the right thing to do," he told the incredulous trio.

The congregation joyfully accepted the land with the understanding it would pay the $30,000 mortgage on the property. To manage this, the members incorporated as the Orchard Hills Community Development Association with plans to develop a twenty- to thirty-unit housing project under the U.S. Department of Agriculture's rural, low-income housing program.

Capt. Haraughty extols the efforts of the local USDA officials, Marion V. Baker and A. C. Manson: "They really went out of their way to help make this a success. They are good Christian laymen, and they don't leave that at home when they go to the office."

Capt. Haraughty also has kind words for the contractor who dug the needed well, the engineers who prepared the land development plan for county approval, the contractor who ordered and erected the prefab houses at Orchard Hills. "They all saw what we were doing was good and right, and they worked along with us on faith. They knew we wouldn't have the money if things didn't work out, but they went right ahead so that things did work out."

But John Haraughty's favorite story is about the emergency grant from the Presiding Bishop's Fund.

"This spring a lot of folks got laid off from their jobs in nearby Lynchburg. With our own orchard, plus the two others where we could have all the peaches we could gather, we needed manpower; but we had nothing to pay them with, nor did we have money for the equipment and sprays we needed if we were going to have anything to harvest. Things were real tight since the unemployment checks were delayed around here.

"So I called Woody Carter (the Church's social affairs officer) in New York City and explained our problems. Woody deals with problems in Appalachia, and he knows us. So he told me to write a request, which we did, and about fifty people signed it. The bishop gave it the finest endorsement and then, wouldn't you know, it got lost in the mail.

"Well, I called Woody again and said we'd send the diocese's copy, but he said he couldn't do much right then since the Presiding Bishop was out of the office until Monday, but did we want an emergency check? It was like Thursday or Friday afternoon, and I said I guessed we could wait.

"By Monday I really had misgivings. How fast could something like that go? When I collected the mail Tuesday morning and found a $6,000 check from New York, I can tell you I was stunned. Lucian and Gene were with me, and when we saw that check, we just all of us went right into the church and got down on our knees.

"A lot of people think the Church doesn't concern itself about requests like ours. But here were people getting hungry and going to stay hungry if the orchards weren't worked, and there came the money so fast, so very fast."

He shakes his head, remembering, and adds, "Do you know, no one can remember how we came up with the $6,000 figure. But it paid every worker $50 weekly for grocery money, bought the stuff we needed, and lasted just exactly 'til the early peaches came in. Isn't that amazing?"

It is. But the people of St. Paul's have done amazing things.

Like building a ball field on top of a mountain.

Or making enough good food, handmade baskets, and bright country quilts to turn a four-figure profit from an annual fall bazaar.

Or enjoying the first homes they've ever owned with all the modern conveniences.

Or learning about running their own business when for generations they've worked for others.

Or working hard to continue Bible study or other Christian education after a full day of hard physical labor.

And in spite of the accomplishments so far, this is just the beginning for St. Paul's. Around Orchard Hills many sentences start, "When we get the money, we're going to . . . ," or "When we finish here, then we'll start . . . "

And how does it all get done? Maybe we can find a clue in the fact that John Haraughty's world isn't peopled by government officials, church bureaucrats, land developers, and bankers but first of all by Christians. He explains, "When I go to Christian men and women with a project that needs doing, I don't want them to tell me the reasons it can't be done. I want them to tell me the ways it can be done."

And for St. Paul's and John Haraughty, those people just sit right down and figure out a way.

One Family:

Finding Joy in the Midst of Loss

by John Reedy

Every Christmas season, no matter how preoccupied I am with all the usual rush of details, I always find some time to be alone, to be quiet, to look back.

A couple of years ago, it was a full Christmas Eve alone, in the empty home of some friends, a couple who had gone out to deliver gifts and found it impossible to break away.

There is the subdued lighting of their decorated family room, looking out at the reflections of neighbors' colored lights on the snow, listening to Christmas music, the memories came back—my life, my experience, my friends became a stream instead of a succession of isolated segments.

More often, it's a quiet weekend or a long evening alone in my office, gradually stretching out what was intended as a short break from writing all those Christmas letters and cards which bring back people, places, shared experience from my childhood, my days in the seminary, and the early years of my priesthood.

There is a flood of memories, but there is one which always comes back, which always stands out, which has a special significance I've never been able to formulate to my own satisfaction.

It was about eight o'clock in the morning on another Christmas Eve, about a dozen years ago.

Though our offices were closed, I had come over to make use of some of the undisturbed time to clear a clutter of details from my desk. The phone startled me. No one should have been calling at that time, on that day.

The voice was familiar. It was the high school-aged daughter, the eldest child, of a family of friends. A couple of years before I had come to know this family well while the parents and I struggled through a period of religous instruction. They were serious about their religious search, unwilling to accept easy formulas.

Over the phone Judy's voice was strained. "Father," she said, "Dad asked me to call you. We just found Rob. He's dead!"

Perhaps it was the early hour. More likely, it was the complete surprise. I just couldn't function. Instead, I found myself falling back on those routine formulas we use. "Is there anything I can do?" "I'll pray for all of you. . . ."

She said, "No, there's nothing. Dad just wanted me to let you know."

The conversation ended and I sat there bewildered. Robbie was their baby, a beautiful, wonderfully healthy 13-month-old baby. There had been a long gap between the older three children and Robbie's birth, and the entire family idolized him, even though they were now awaiting the birth of another child.

Gradually, the realization began to seep into my understanding. "Good God," I thought. "It must have just happened; they must have just found him."

I grabbed the old jacket I had worn to the office that morning and drove over to their home.

The door opened and I'll never forget that scene. It was as I had thought. All the family were still in their nightclothes. Their lovely, warm home was decorated for Christmas. The tree was lit and surrounded with gifts.

Dick, the father, looked up at me with tears, with agony in his eyes. He sat holding the baby's body.

Lois, the mother, came to me. There was nothing either of us could say. I held her while in the back of my mind I begged God that this shock should not endanger the child she was carrying.

Finally, we began to talk the kind of halting, strained talk that goes on at a surface level when people are unable to say what they are really feeling.

The baby had seemed perfectly healthy the night before when he was put to bed. Although he had signs of what seemed a slight cold, there was nothing that caused concern. (Later, the doctor said it was a fast-acting kind of pneumonia; even if Rob had been in the hospital, the doctor said, there was little they could have done for him.)

In the early morning someone had routinely checked on him—and then their lives fell apart.

We sat there together, but each was isolated in a personal misery. The father, the mother, the two young daughters, and the younger son. And the priest who felt he should be able to offer some kind of support, some kind of ministry, only to find himself choking on all those familiar formulas which at this moment seemed irrelevant to, if not a profanation of, the grief suffered by people.

And the baby, there in his father's arms.

We waited, and waited, as mourning people always do. No one wanted to break the moment. Even if we had wanted to do so, no one would have known how.

Finally, after what seemed hours of waiting, the undertaker came. And then came still another throb of torment. The father was unwilling to hand over the body of his infant son to a stranger.

What then happened grew out of my earlier visits to their home. Tiny children have always intimidated me. I have never been around babies long enough to get used to them. They always seem too fragile to handle and I have a fear that in my awkwardness I might somehow injure them. And so, in spite of constant encouragement and teasing, I had never held Robbie. "Wait until he's two," I would say. "Then he can begin to defend himself."

But at this moment, with the undertaker standing awkward and uncertain in their living room, with Dick blindly unwilling to part with his son's body, Lois somehow found the right thing to say to her husband.

"Dick, let Father take Robbie. He'll hold him now."

I caught my breath; I wasn't ready for that.

There was a long moment of no response. Then Dick slowly held the baby's body out for me to take.

My eyes were so filled that I could hardly see to follow the undertaker to the door. We walked outside the house. He closed the door and I handed the tiny body to him.

He left and I went back to the family. Just to be with them for a time.

The next afternoon, Christmas Day, only the parents, their own parents, their three children and I went over to the funeral home. Just one member of the staff was present. Because of the day, it seemed inappropriate that the establishment should be open at all. And also because of the day, the distinctive funeral home atmosphere—the odor, the subdued lighting, the muffled sound—seemed horribly inappropriate.

We sat before the coffin, which because of its size looked like some grotesque toy. We talked quietly, in fragments, with long silences. The grandparents were as stunned and as helpless as I.

But I began to sense something about this family. The shock and sorrow were, of course, unimaginable. But something else was beginning to emerge, something which I didn't recognize at first—a quality or tone which didn't quite fit the utter desolation I expected to find in them.

Along with the tears and the grief, there was more composure, more control, than I thought would be possible. In words, glances, embraces, there were currents going between Dick and Lois and between them and their children. All of them seemed to draw support from these currents.

Later I realized that this was the first sign of a family strength at a time when I would have thought strength would be impossible.

We remained at the funeral home for an hour or so and finally left. They knew I was expected at another home for a Christmas dinner and they insisted that I go ahead, while they, with their parents and children, returned to their own home.

The transition from that near empty funeral home to the noisy, jumbled celebration of a happy family was the greatest emotional transition I have ever encountered. In fact, I didn't manage it very well. During moments when I was not involved in conversation, I would find my thoughts and emotions drifting off across town to that other family, their home decorated for joy, filled with grief. I contributed little to the gaiety of the family with whom I shared that Christmas.

It had been decided that Robbie's funeral would be held as soon as possible, the morning after Christmas. I was asked to offer the Mass.

When I thought about the timing and the fact that there had been no time for any public notice in the newspapers, I expected the service to be similar to our visit to the funeral home, just the family and a few of their closest friends.

To my surprise, the church was almost filled. There had been a lot of telephoning in that parish on Christmas Eve and on Christmas Day.

When the family arrived at the church, I met them. Dick took me aside and said, "Father, we'd like to have the casket open during the Mass."

I was stunned. No family had ever made this request to me before.

I tried to persuade him to change his mind. "Dick, all of you have suffered enough, this will tear you apart."

But there was no uncertainty in him. "No," he said, "we all talked this over. It's what we want."

So I went over to the undertaker and told him of the request. He said, "Oh, no, Father. We don't do that. It's against the policy of the parishes here."

We argued about it. The pastor happened to be in the hospital and the undertaker wanted to know who was going to take responsibility for the decision.

"I'll take the responsibility," I said. "With what this family is going through, the only thing I care about is their feelings."

Reluctantly, he agreed. I don't know whether he expected the bishop to suspend me or boycott his firm. Neither possibility bothered me much at that moment.

When I came out to the altar to begin the Mass, my eyes couldn't avoid the tiny casket. Robbie lay there dressed in a suspendered kind of playsuit, looking as beautiful and healthy as ever.

All through the Mass, whenever I looked up, my gaze returned to the infant who seemed to be sleeping peacefully, unaware of all these people, all this solemnity, all this emotion.

And each time, when I pulled my eyes away from the baby, they would be drawn over to the parents, the sisters, and brother. There was no way I could comprehend what they were experiencing but my sympathy flowed out to them. And each time, my eyes filled up, producing some long pauses before I could again focus on the words of the missal.

At the end of the Mass I came down to the communion rail, just a few feet in front of the open casket and spoke. Neither immediately afterwards nor now can I remember what I said—except for one thing.

I said that in searching for words which could give some support to these friends of mine, I had reviewed all the formulas of faith and hope to which my life was committed. And all of them seemed grossly inappropriate. Not because they were untrue or meaningless—because I firmly believed in them—but because all of these truths seemed to speak to the mind. And this family was not hurting in their minds; they were hurting in their emotions. With such a hurt, all we could do was be present, grieve with them, try to make known our love for them.

Finally, it ended. I remember little about the ceremony at the grave, but when I finished speaking in the church the family arose and came out into the aisle beside the casket.

They stood there for a moment. Then the father, the mother, and each of the children bent over, kissed the infant, and turned and walked to the rear of the church.

And through badly blurred vision I somehow followed the servers back into the sacristy to unvest.

Later in the day, back at my office, one of my co-workers who was also a friend of the family came in to see me. He had been at the funeral.

Though he is emotional, he is one of those men who likes to project an image of being breezy and hard-nosed. None of that image was present in our subdued conversation.

He seemed bewildered by his own emotions. "God," he said, "if anyone had ever told me that the funeral of a baby—at Christmas time—could be beautiful, I would have told him he was out of his mind."

He paused, then added softly, "But it *was* beautiful!"

Every year, during one of those quiet times before Christmas, this is one of the memories which flows back, in all its details.

As I said earlier, I've tried to sort out and understand some of the many perceptions and responses which were churning around inside me during that time. I haven't fully succeeded, but here are some of the reflections which this process has produced.

First, there was the shocking mystery of a cruel suffering I couldn't begin to explain. You can say all you want about God taking Robbie to a happiness even greater than he could have known in his family. In faith I believe that. But humanly, looking at this child and his family, it sounds like something said in a language I never learned.

Why give this baby to his family for only 13 months? Why, of all times, on Christmas Eve, a day warm and rich with family love and joy and anticipation?

Through the years, of course, I've seen other shocking tragedies come into lives I have known, suffering and loss which was outside the normal expectations of our lives, tearing at good, sensitive people in a way which seems almost whimsically cruel. But in the twenty-two years of my priesthood, no other tragedy hit me quite as hard as Robbie's death in those circumstances.

And none of those formulas from theology or spiritual reading provided an explanation which makes sense to me.

Only the phrase, "the mystery of the Cross," suggests that those who profess to follow Christ do, in fact, accept a vulnerability beyond our expectations.

It is an openness to God's will, a fierce commitment to believe in his love, no matter how difficult it might be to discern the signs of that love in our lives.

And it is truly mysterious, impenetrable by all our human efforts to make sense of it. Why does such a thing happen to these lives when other Christians, the same kind of people, never encounter anything like it?

While I was completely incapable of *understanding* the mystery of the suffering my friends endured, I was able to perceive signs that beyond the cloud of pain, loss, and bewilderment, beyond the cross, the loving Father was present.

How else could anyone understand the strength and the faith of this family? It's difficult to use ordinary words to describe the human reality. It was an acceptance not of their baby's sudden death, but of the fact that somehow even such a horrible loss has meaning and purpose in the providence of a loving God.

There was the extraordinary unity and strength which the family drew from each other. The other children were then fairly young, but they took on a remarkable maturity during those days in sharing the suffering and contributing to the support the parents found in each other and in them.

During recent years, when much religious thought and energy has gone into social causes, I've thought about the bleak reality described by that phrase, the mystery of the cross.

There's no doubt in my mind that the gospel vocation calls us to respond to social need; but there's also no doubt that the reality of this vocation goes beyond the politics and economics of social reform.

Even in a just, loving society, the mysterious ways of God would leave people just as bewildered. They would still encounter the real possibility of being stripped raw, of being faced with the unavoidable choice: accept the reality of a loving God no matter where it might lead, or plunge into bitterness and despair.

On another line of reflection, this experience generated some humbling thoughts about my own faith, about the ministry of my priesthood.

I couldn't walk away from my participation in this family's suffering without wondering how my own faith, so easily professed, would have survived if this had been my child.

The things in my life which I described as disappointments and hardships seem trivial when compared to such naked suffering.

Also humbling was the recognition of just how incidental, how instrumental, my ministry to them had been.

I went back over all the time we had spent together during that course of instructions. Most of my time was spent on all those details we were expected to cover in such presentations, everything from indulgences to Lenten fast and abstinence, to the whole catalogue of mortal and venial sins.

In one of our first discussions, Lois was frank in her comment, "Father, I guess I just don't want to be a Catholic. There are a lot of things about Catholic life and belief that I just don't like."

I felt rather smug about my answer. I told her, "There are a lot of things about Catholic life that I don't like either. If I felt I had a choice, I'm sure I could find a religious belief that would be more attractive."

They pushed me hard, challenging and questioning, sending me back to reference books. Then suddenly, without any reference to what we were discussing, it all changed. It became, "You don't have to prove all that. Just tell us what the church teaches. We accept the church and its teachings."

It was obvious that the significant change which had occurred was between God and these people. As far as the reality of that change was concerned I could have been juggling apples instead of explaining indulgences.

Though the realization shook any vanity I had in my effectiveness as a catechist, it was also reassuring during a time when a lot of priests were having second thoughts about the effectiveness of what they were doing.

To me, the basic question came to be not whether I was achieving the maximum effectiveness that could be drawn from my personality, ability, and training. Instead, it was a matter of being available, with all my limitations, to serve as an instrument as God carries on his mysterious dealings with the people whom I encounter.

And that awareness was immeasurably deepened as I watched the profound religious faith of this family in their suffering and loss. There was no doubt in my mind, nor in the minds of their friends, I believe, that their extraordinary ability to endure and grow through this loss was rooted in their faith in God and in each other.

Where does such a perspective come from? Certainly not from the kind of explanation I had offered. Again, I saw very clearly my role as instrument while the basic relationship developed between God and the individuals.

Such recognition puts the success or failure of human projects in a different perspective. For me, it has been a reassuring perspective.

Finally, looking at this family in its happiness and warmth, in its loss and suffering and seeing its humanity infused with a religious response to God, I can see the wonder of the Incarnation in a new reality.

Scripture doesn't say much about the family life of Jesus, but the fact that God chose to redeem humanity through this universal human experience has to be important. It requires people to use their understanding of family life as a way of looking at God's plan.

While one shouldn't reject the significance of those religious persons who have been recognized for their wisdom, austerity, or leadership, the reality of the Lord's coming into the world suggests that God is calling for a more ordinary response.

Certainly the family and friends of Jesus knew the ordinary joys of warmth and celebration, rejoicing in the joys of those whom they loved.

They also knew the reality of loss, the human bewilderment at what must have been seen as unjustified suffering.

In all of this human experience of Jesus, which is shared in varying degrees by most families, the immediate design of God was being worked out.

Surely this says that for most people a loving response to the Father is to be expressed not in deep theological speculation or in extraordinary commitments but in the ordinary patterns of family relationships: service to others through work, in openness and response to friends and others whose needs become evident.

At a time when many people seem distressed because they can't find meaning and achievement in their lives, this memory of Christmas seems to say: the meaning is in the living itself. Don't be blinded by regret over accomplishments unattained. Open your eyes and your lives to the God revealed in a newborn infant, in a family called Holy, in a teacher's modest accomplishment, in a man's suffering and death accepted as God's mysterious will.

None of these reflections is very startling or profound, but all are much more real to me for having emerged from the reality of that Christmas loss suffered by my friends.

In the intervening years, their lives have gone on. All three of the children who shared that Christmas are grown and married. Two younger children are at home with Dick and Lois.

Curiously, though I'm sure our lives are intimately linked through the sharing of that tragedy, I don't see them very frequently. When we do get together I have the feeling that all of us are very conscious of that moment which was too painful and too rich to be the subject of ordinary reminiscence.

This is the first time I've written about it, the first time I've tried to express to them and to others what it meant to me.

I hope they will understand what I've said, and what I've left unsaid.

Judith Cox:

God Shapes Her Destiny

by Judith Kay Cox

I pick up the blob of clay and squeeze it. The cool, moist substance squishes between my fingers. Excitement ripples through my body. For nearly three quarters of a century I have sculpted with clay, and each time I begin a new piece this feeling overwhelms me.

I become possessed by the possibilities held prisoner in the clay and begin feverishly to unleash them. I turn blob to beauty using the knarled, slow-moving hands once quick and steady. In my youth I could sculpt a piece in hours; now it takes days, sometimes weeks, to finish one. Now I know patience precedes perfection.

When I lost my eyesight I found insight. This changed me from just another sculptor to an artist. A sculpted object may be a thing of visual beauty, but an object of art arouses other senses and emotions as well.

I pinch. I smooth. I poke. I smooth. I mold. I smooth.

The clock chimes three. My two granddaughters are stopping by after school for tea and cookies.

Each day they come by to make sure I'm all right. In their eyes I am very old and tomorrow is uncertain. Since they are young and eager for living, their futures are uncertain. After we chat I am sure they are all right, and I hope I have assured them that I am.

They leave. I feel the urge to work again and continue slowly. Not rushing from goal to goal but taking my time, I enjoy each moment as a treasure God has given me. I am not possessed by the thought of reaching a goal. What happens on the way is more important than the destination, except the ultimate one, eternity. I relax knowing that my future is in the hands of The Artist, our Creator, God.

I pinch. I smooth. I poke. I smooth. I mold. I smooth.

Beauty is being born again in my hands.

Dorothy Russell:

A Mighty Mite
Who Mends Men

by Colin Willis

Dorothy Russell, the diminutive director of the Men's Service Centre of the United Church's Montreal City Mission, interrupts a conversation one morning with an urgent "just a minute" and crosses to the hall to an overcoated figure who is breaking one of the few house rules. Head back, he has a bottle of booze to his lips.

She hurries with a slightly lopsided walk, a souvenir of polio when she was very young. A moment later, hand on his elbow, she leads him an unprotesting thirty-five yards to the door. He was drunk. And almost six feet tall. She is four-feet-eleven.

Quite unruffled, she comes back seconds afterwards. "Drinking is one thing I won't allow," she says perkily in a slightly English-accented voice. "It is the main reason why people are here and I won't have them doing it in the mission."

Dot, as she is generally known outside the mission, Sister by "my boys" within it, or Mrs. Russell to the grocer, is an improbable person to run entirely on her own Montreal's only day refuge for down-and-outs, up to 350 of them a day with no homes, no jobs, and no place else to go for the day.

She is the wrong size for one thing. And from the wrong background, for another. "A good Montreal family" sounds snobbish, but that is where she comes from. Music study at McGill University preceded a ten-year job as secretary to the late Rev. Norman Rawson of St. James Church, Montreal. Then came a year with the United Church assisting immigrants before improbably throwing in her lot with life at the bottom of the human ladder.

Even those who know her well still cannot believe it. "What," a voice asked her after she had given a talk to the Montreal Presbytery, "are *you* doing down there with those bums, Dot?"

"Ladies and gentlemen," she retorted reprovingly in evangelical style, ignoring the real question, "we do not think of them in terms of bums, but as children of God, because you can't totally separate a child from its father."

Thrusting fist into palm for emphasis, she recalls fondly: "*That* stopped them in their tracks."

Indeed. But though it may have been an uncharitable question, it was certainly a very human one.

For "down there" is not the sort of place you would expect a middle-aged, McGill-educated woman to have spent six years of her life. It is a very large, rather dingy, partitioned room over a fish market just off St. Lawrence Boulevard—the traditional dividing line between French- and English-Canada.

And though it is still an ideal spot for a day mission, it is a most unlikely one for Dot, who answers another inevitable question with a firm: "I have never, never been threatened." Does she protest too much, you wonder? For even if she had been, you doubt if she would admit it. Her loyalty to "my family" (one of two; she also has a husband and two married sons) is mother-like in its protective intensity.

"Our Christian attitude," she defines her position, characteristically using the editorial plural, "is reaching out to the goodness in these men. And in reaching out you get good."

It is a reciprocated faith. "You are worse than a mother to me," someone joshes her. "Oh, Sister," exclaims another, "it is just like home here." It can conjure up an odd look of childish devotion.

So you are not surprised when the police, whom she has called only once, for a medical emergency, say: "Her greatest protection on skid row is skid row itself."

Dot is a fighter in a world that has, for whatever reason, largely given up the fight. She seems to be able to put stuffing into the most downcast. She offers hope in an essentially hopeless world, comfort of the broadest kind. And yet though life in this world is usually cabbage-like, for many it can be not unhappy.

She loathes the word *bum*. Yet Dot is no sentimentalist; she could never manage the harsh realities of the mission if she were. Bums there are and criminals, too. Everything from murder downwards, most of it petty in intent if not in result.

What annoys her is the indifferent contempt the word's use normally implies. Rather evasively she will even concede: "We know they exist, people who could work but don't." But in the same breath she will rush to point out this man with lung cancer, that one an outpatient from a mental hospital. Drink is the tip of an iceberg, and leave you to see for yourself that maybe a quarter are too old, too obviously sick, to do anything.

Average age is the ominous fifty. They do not even make particularly energetic panhandlers. "A lot are going down without realizing it. Nearly all are loners. Many have been married. But I have never," she adds significantly, "been asked to write a letter of reconciliation."

Which is one way of saying that the Montreal mission is very much like any other. But apart from being run by a woman it is different in one important way: Three quarters of its users are French Canadians. Dot thus speaks more French than English. Most of the men are products of pre-"Quiet Revolution" Quebec education, and consequently more than usual are functional illiterates.

The combination could be, in a manner of speaking, an explosive one. The pride of a down-and-out can be touchy, even if it is only the pride of defeat. And, in a place where arguments can flare over nothing, it calls for the skill of a diplomat to handle them. Add, too, the French resentment of the English. So Dot's success becomes a tribute to her superb tact.

And to the woman's touch: "It doesn't challenge them," she feels.

At the mission's opening around nine she can be greeted by a hungry crowd of as many as 100 dishevelled men, many of whom have slept "rough."

There are 7,500 square feet of the mission to be swept for a start, the sweepers urged on by such popular hymns as "Onward Christian Soldiers."

There are razors for unshaven beards, needle and thread for torn clothes . . . and fresh clothes handed out on a highly selective basis from the "mini department store": *highly* selective because they are only too likely to be traded for the next drink. There are clean handkerchiefs, made in their hundreds by the United Church Women and the men themselves, for any who want them.

"They do more for a man's self-respect than anything I know," says Dot the psychologist.

Then come, in her vivid phrasing, "quantities of clear, brilliant, sparkling tea, tremendously remedial for men who are alcoholics." There are games to play, old magazines and newspapers to read.

Lunch is what Dot calls "the coffee kitchen." In truth it is not much more than that. Supplies come from stores, institutions and individuals. Depending on the world's kindness that day, it is usually soup, sandwich, coffee, and a cake. Dot tends to be philosophical about the unpredictable quantities. It is her pride, though, that donors give enough so that the mission has to spend only about $30 a month on supplies. Consequently, the annual cost of the work, paid for by the United Church's Board of Home Missions, is kept to around $14,000.

The afternoon is the morning in reverse, tea and a final sweep up, until closing around five. For Dot it is a busy day filled with supervising, administering the mission, hustling up supplies, locating jobs, acting as nurse, confidant, and adviser.

Many of the users have incomes of some sort, largely pensions and welfare. Dot can be harsh about these welfare payments. " . . . far too much money is often being given and too easily received. . . . A man should help himself and should be helped to help himself." On pay days the mission can be almost empty.

Though she might chide a man she never hustles him about work. She has many sympathetic contacts in town and will sometimes get more job offers than she can fill. In a recent week she fixed up ten. In a year she might arrange 50 times that many. She has sent grape pickers off to California, tobacco strippers to Ontario. Though the money may end up buying rubbing alcohol, it has not, at least, been "too easily received."

Unlike elsewhere in town, no one has to pray, as it were, for their suppers. But on Sundays there is a voluntary service. It is the mission's most popular event except for Christmas dinner. Up to 225 will squeeze themselves in.

Gifts come Dot's way from the men, small things: a crucifix possibly, earrings, stockings. One, Dot recalls with a grin, was a bottle of gin and the donor was horrified when he learned she had tipped it down the sink. "But a drop of gin would do you good," he expostulated.

The empty bottle has been kept, however, as has the occasional note of appreciation. "I am still sober," reads one, "and this I owe to you. . . . I want to thank you for everything . . . so that I could go to work with some clothes."

Dot is normally a person of immense good humor, a beaver for work, as energetic as a bag full of monkeys. She is also very independent. "I don't know how anyone manages to live with her," says an admiring friend.

She is in constant demand as a speaker. In a recent week she gave four talks, one of them a sermon at a church seventy-five miles away. A great burner of candles at both ends with apparently no sense of time, she might, she thinks, clock up seventy hours of work a week.

Occasionally, though, she will sit in the mission's reception office, her lively grey-blue eyes scanning the shelf of shopping bags holding the men's sole possessions, the drawer with the magical handkerchiefs, the counter that is part confessional, part advisory clinic, and admit to feeling a bit depressed. It is quite a confession itself from this normally indomitable woman.

The best cure is a lost face appearing around the corner. It is usually smiling.

At Work in a Nursing Home:

He Is Never "Done" with His Patients

by Richard Hubbard

The first time I walked into a nursing home, my nose was assaulted wih the combined odor of urine, medicine, and sweat. I was greeted at the door by a thin, graying, elderly patient who said, "Hi, did you come to take me home?"

I mumbled a "No," assuming that the old man was totally confused. And I walked by, trying not to look at the patients around me.

After a while, I learned that the old man was more lonely than confused, and that the offensive odor was not the smell of old people, but the characteristic smell of nursing homes.

I also noticed an unnatural silence in the house. Only the occasional shriek or shouting of a name would break through the quiet bustling of the nurses. With so many people gathered in so small a place, I wondered why there was so little conversation. What I didn't realize then was that in order to have a conversation, you first need something to talk about, and then someone to listen to you. Both of these essentials were missing in the home.

Even at the most sociable time of the day, the dinner hour, the silence prevailed. The policy was that as many patients as possible were to be taken to the dining room each night for supper. But it was left to the aides to decide who would go to dinner and who would remain in bed. And often the patients taken to the dining hall were the ones easiest to handle rather than the ones who might need company the most.

But what happened in the dining room itself was even more eerie. The four men or women at each table ate in complete silence. I was stunned. The aides brought the trays of food in silently, cut the meat for those who needed help, and left. They seemed to promote the silence.

After two days of this not-very gainful employment, I decided something had to be done. At the next meal, I seated both men and women at every table, first asking them if there was any particular place they would like to sit (this eventually grew into a custom of making reservations for dinner). And I seated the patients with a great show of etiquette. That alone seemed to promote talking. But the conversation increased most markedly with the way I served dinner in waiter-like fashion, balancing the tray on one hand over my head. I then announced the menu, placed the tray carefully, and often returned to the table to see if everything was satisfactory. Almost instantaneously people had something to talk about. For some it was the food, for others it was that "crazy orderly," and for others the simple opportunity for conversation in a normal social gathering of men and women.

With this sort of approach to mealtime, the diners began to feel free to ask me for more sugar or an extra slice of bread, or even to complain to me about the food (the complaints were not wholly unjustified). It seemed to me that the effort to make their meals a personal event, not just an institutional routine, improved both the appetites and the dispositions of many of the patients.

In my first week on the job a woman in a wheelchair drew up, pointing to me and shouting, "Whiskers on the moon, whiskers on the moon," and then wheeled away, laughing.

A few weeks earlier, I might have thought she was crazy. Now, out of curiosity, I stopped the woman and asked her why she had used the phrase.

"Well, when I was little, as soon as the boys started getting whiskers for the first time, we'd tease them by shouting that. You got a full beard, so I figured I'd give it to you good. You ain't mad, are you?"

"No," I replied, "just curious."

"Good for you," she exclaimed and pinched me as she wheeled away.

That was the beginning of one of my first friendships in the home. It might have ended where it began, as just another "crazy-old-lady story," had I not asked a simple question.

On another day, I passed a patient who was shouting nonsense syllables and constantly folding and re-folding an old towel. This, I thought, could certainly be labeled bizarre behavior. But I stopped and introduced myself to see what would happen.

"Excuse me," I said, "my name is Richard."

"My name is Edna," she replied. "You know, you're quite an interesting stimulus in this environment."

Edna may have been confused, but she had an extraordinary vocabulary, could speak in complete sentences, and could carry on a conversation.

Unfortunately, I wasn't able to find out from her how she had come by her habit of towel-folding and her large vocabularly. I might have checked her patient resumé. There was no social worker connected with the home.

Ultimately, from some of her visitors, I found out that Edna had once been a nurse in a large hospital. This not only provided a clue to her remarkable vocabulary but suggested that her towel-folding behavior was a carry-over from hospital sterile techniques.

Armed with this knowledge I tried to ask Edna for nursing hints, and for help in folding some materials we used in the home. But time and confusion had won out. She had been left to play with her rag too long. I still wonder what might have happened if a social worker had seen her when she arrived.

Part of the reason no one ever found out about Edna was because she was readily labeled as a "baby," babbling and playing with a rag.

Treatment of old people as children is a constant problem, especially in nursing homes, but in society as well. But even if the analogy of old age to childhood were entirely accurate, the logical conclusions are ignored. For instance, a child does not learn to eat, walk, and get along with others all at once. Nor does an elderly person lose all these powers at once—that is, unless one is forced to lose them.

Often the patient's body is no longer willing to let him control his bladder or to walk. And the nursing home itself takes away the right to eat, to sleep, and to come and go as the resident pleases. Removal of the "right to decide" removes much of the patient's self-esteem.

One patient may be able to get ready for bed herself if she is allowed an hour's time. But an aide assigned to see that ten patients are in bed in two hours doesn't have the time to *assist* them. She only has time to take over and "put them to bed."

But the aide who says to a few patients, "Let me know when you're tired," instead of "It's time for bed," may find herself doing less work instead of more. If a patient is allowed to decide when he is tired, he might also be able to get into bed by himself.

In this, as in many other matters, the way that seems convenient for the staff may not be best for the residents. At the sign of their first fall, for example, patients are frequently strapped in a chair. A patient strapped to a chair won't fall again. He won't walk again, either.

The same is true for the first wet bed. This commonly leads to diapers or catheterization for the offender. Both methods will keep the bed dry; and both methods will hasten the loss of bladder control.

A resident of a home for the aged is well aware of whether he is being treated as a person or as just a "patient." An aide who constantly thinks in terms of "patients" becomes a caretaker rather than an aid to therapy. A caretaker knows when she is "done" with a patient; she does things to her patient, not with him. Though old age wears away at physical abilities, it does not diminish a person's sensitivity.

Aged people often feel imprisoned by nursing homes and also by their bodies. As one of my friends, Johnny, said to me three days before he died, "If this ain't no prison, how come the only way out of here is to die?"

It is no great wonder then, that the aged often try to leave the institution and go "home." Many of them leave out of loneliness, perhaps after a visit from someone they used to know.

When residents do attempt to leave, it seems far better—from what I've seen—to let them proceed with their attempt. Certainly, it does not help an aide to rush up in panic, grab the patient, and yell, "Hey, where do you think you're going?"

Fortunately, this was not the approach used late one night when one of the residents, a man named Loyal, passed the reception desk and said, "Good night folks, I'm going to work."

One of the aides walked up to him and said, "I think you're confused, Loyal. You're retired now, and there's no reason to go to work. Why don't you stay here with us?"

"I'm not confused," Loyal said, "I got to go to work and drive the trucks."

"But, Loyal, you're retired from trucking now. Don't worry about making it to work. I'd hate to see you leave in this weather without a car," the aide said.

"Well, maybe you're right," Loyal answered.

What is noteworthy is what the aide didn't do. He didn't try to deceive Loyal with doubletalk, another damaging strategy often used on confused residents. A doubletalker would have simply told Loyal, "The boss called up and said you can have the night off, so why don't you go to bed?" Had Loyal pressed for details, such an aide would have invented them, greatly adding to Loyal's confusion.

When another resident, Julie, was lying on the front lawn of the nursing home one day, two aides and a nurse came up and tried to coax her to come in by suggesting she would miss dinner. Julie had told them that she was resting before walking home and that she was getting irritated with people in white looking down at her.

Another aide, Ann—a friend of Julie's—came along, asked for some time alone with Julie, and (much to the nurse's dismay) lay down on the grass beside her.

"Julie," Ann asked, "what's going on out here? You trying to get a sun tan?"

"I'm just resting before I go home," Julie said, still angry.

"Why do you want to go home?"

" 'Cause I'm lonely."

"Don't your folks come to see you almost every night? Aren't they coming tonight?"

"Yes, but I don't like staying here," Julie said.

"I don't blame you for that, Julie. But at least you get company. That's more than a lot of folks up here get. Besides, we can take pretty good care of you here. And who would dance with me if you left?"

"Ann, you're crazy!"

"Maybe so, but if we don't go inside the neighbors are sure gonna talk."

"Ann, go on—you're so crazy."

"Would you like to talk to your folks about wanting to go home?"

"Yes," Julie said.

"Well, then, we'll do that. But right now, let's go eat."

It is obvious that to Ann, Julie was more than just a "patient." Ann later told the family about the episode, and they were forced to face themselves and the reasons why they had placed Julie in the nursing home.

Easter People:

Freed to Be Love's Captives

by Jack Moore

Grey and dreary, it is a depressing day. Actually, I feel my spirit drooping and my enthusiasm for life smothering in the thick glumness of the weather.

Then the rain stops. Suddenly and unexpectedly. Not according to predictions. The clouds are brushed aside by impertinent breezes. The sun peeks out, ducks in, and then breaks through with an irresistible smile.

The day starts to sparkle and there's a fresh message vibrating through my nervous system. It's great to be alive.

And know the meaning of Easter.

In one corner of the room a little boy is squatting and squalling. Alternating between wails of despair and sobs of distress. Fighting off every attempt by the anxious adults to comfort him. At least to shush him.

In the midst of this drama, his mother returns. Coming through the nursery door with her arms reaching out for him and a loving smile on her familiar face.

Racing across the room, he throws himself against her and buries his face in her lap. Slowly, gradually, his little heart stops its wild beating. He knows he is safe.

The meaning of Easter.

I've just come from the hospital and a tumor of grief is growing within me.

My friend is dead. Only yesterday he was talking of going home. Where there had been so much hope and determination, now there is nothing. Death has ended his life, our relationship.

Then I remember.

Standing beside his bed for the last time, I was having trouble with my emotions. Smiling, he squeezed my hand and said, "I'll always be with you. No matter what."

Easter.

Tiredness gathering in the corners of my eyes and crawling along the laugh lines toward my temples was jarred off course by that sound of sounds. The telephone ringing.

"Whatcha doing? Why aren't you home? Tried to get you there and they said you'd be late."

The voice, at first, was only vaguely familiar. Then, with an explosion of deep feelings, I recognized it. A cousin, more like a brother, from a long way off and a long time ago.

"I'm at the airport," he said. "Have only an hour between flights."

It wasn't much, but it was something. It was seeing again. Touching. Hurriedly swapping family data. Then, with tears stinging my eyes, it was watching his plane disappear into the night.

Easter is many things.

Wherever love lights and lightens my life. And yours.

Wherever there is a new beginning. A renewing of meanings. A flush of virgin hope in the midst of old hurts and old failures.

That is Easter.

Whenever there is a balm for the wounds of my spirit, a salve for those cuts and gashes that are mostly self-inflicted.

Whenever there is a healing lotion for the betrayals of the Judas in me, for the denials that I share with Peter, and for my countless desertions in the face of public pressure.

>That, my friends, is Easter.
>Ah, now I see it more clearly.
>What I do is let myself be free.
>Free to be captive to the love of God.
>In Jesus the Christ.
>That makes Easter possible for me.
>In all my living.
>And dying.
>And living again.

Thank You, God for . . .

by Gail Pallotta

The fresh summer breeze
That rustles through the trees
And wraps our hearts with love

The warmth of sun rays
That brightens up our days
And fills our hearts with cheer

The cool, pleasant rain
That refreshes earth's domain
And gives us peace

The glittering Heaven at night
That makes our darkness light
And lifts our hearts with hope

The young boy, kind and strong
Who helps the old lady
Move her grocery cart along

The middle-aged man, hurried this day,
Taking time to fix the tire
For a lady stranded by the way

The housewife, tired and weary,
Baking cookies for a lonely friend
Whose days are long and dreary

The young couple, just beginning life,
Who think to visit someone ill
Hoping to relieve their strife

The old man, with dreams that are torn,
Who still smiles and says
"Enjoy today. Be happy you were born."

These things
That push our problems away
And make us know
Your love is here to stay.

Acknowledgments

All stories in this book appeared originally as articles in the journals that cooperate through Interchurch Features. Reprint permission has been granted by the publishers. The sources are listed in the order of their appearance in *The Power of One*.

"Nearly Everybody Knows Chris," by Floramae Geiser. *The Lutheran,* September 18, 1974. © *The Lutheran.* Used by permission.

"Amazing Grace at the Met," by Thomas Orrin Bentz. *A.D.,* April, 1975. © *A.D.* Used by permission.

"Esperanza," by Marilynne Hill. *The Disciple,* January 19, 1975. © Christian Board of Publication. Used by permission.

" 'The Lady' Who Made an Impact" by Jean D. Ketchum. *The Disciple,* January 18, 1976. © Christian Board of Publication. Used by permission.

"Make Today Count," by Orville E. Kelly. *A.D.,* January, 1975. © *A.D.* Used by permission.

"Brown Creek Church, Mr. Smith—and Me," by William H. Willimon. *Today,* July, 1974. © United Methodist Publishing House. Reprinted with permission.

"Uncle Gus," from *In a Mirror Dimly,* by Jack Moore. *Presbyterian Survey,* July, 1975. © *Presbyterian Survey.* Used by permission.

"And God Said to Kathryn, 'Go!' " by Kathryn Waller. *The Episcopalian,* September, 1975. © *The Episcopalian.* Used by permission.

"Mummy, the Man From the Church Is Here!" by James Taylor. *The United Church Observer,* October, 1975. Reprinted by permission.

"A Riot Set Her Faith on Fire," by Martha A. Lane. *Today,* August, 1974. © United Methodist Publishing House. Reprinted with permission.

"Ron Schipper: More Than a Football Coach," by Barbara Sagraves. *The Church Herald,* December 26, 1975. © *The Church Herald.* Used by permission.

"My Monday Morning Letters," by Don Jennings. *Today,* February, 1975. © United Methodist Publishing House. Reprinted with permission.

"Mission on a Motorcycle," by A. Jean Lesher. *The Lutheran,* January 1, 1975. © *The Lutheran.* Used by permission.

"Soochow's Friends—and How They Grew," by Andrew Hamilton. *Today,* April, 1975. © United Methodist Publishing House. Reprinted with permission.

"Sometimes We're Happy," by Pauline Miller. *U.S. Catholic,* June, 1975. © Claretian Publications. Used by permission.

"She Turned Her Other Cheek—and Got Hit Again!" by Richard K. Taylor. *The Lutheran,* January 23, 1974. © *The Lutheran.* Used by permission.

"The Gift of Joy," by Marie Coventry. *The United Church Observer,* October, 1971. Reprinted by permission.

"Return of the Revolutionists," by J. Richard Peck. *Today,* June, 1975. © United Methodist Publishing House. Reprinted with permission.

"Lydia Dowler Listens to God," by Nancy Millar. *The United Church Observer,* October, 1975. Reprinted by permission.

"New Homes, Jobs Grow in Old Orchard," by Janette Pierce. *The Episcopalian,* March, 1975. © *The Episcopalian.* Used by permission.

"Sleep in Heavenly Peace," by Father John Reedy, C.S.C. *U.S. Catholic,* December, 1975. © Claretian Publications. Used by permission.

"Treasure of Today," by Judith Kay Cox. *Presbyterian Survey,* August, 1975. © *Presbyterian Survey.* Used by permission.

"The Mighty Mite Who Mends Men," by Colin Willis. *The United Church Observer,* February, 1971. Reprinted by permission.

"Hi, Did You Come to Take Me Home?" by Richard Hubbard. *U.S. Catholic,* August, 1975. © Claretian Publications. Used by permission.

"Easter People," from *In a Mirror Dimly,* by Jack Moore. *Presbyterian Survey,* March, 1975. © *Presbyterian Survey.* Used by permission.

"Thank You, God For . . . " by Gail Pallotta. *Presbyterian Survey,* November, 1975. © *Presbyterian Survey.* Used by permission.